Mindful Meditation Made Easy

Your Step-by-Step Journey

Michael T. Lohr

Table of Contents

Foreword

This book is the culmination of my experiences over the last 25 years. However, it is told in the voice of everyone, because everyone's journey is different. I stumbled into mindful meditation as a last resort in my lifelong battle with depression and anxiety. Those have been gone for a long time now. I probably read 20 or more books to gather all the information found in this book. It is a blueprint, designed to take you through an easy-to-understand, step-by-step method of achieving maximum benefit from your journey. Living mindfully is indescribable; it is the definition of "stopping to smell the roses." If you give it an honest try, you will feel a change in weeks, not months or years. That change will get better and better over time. It doesn't require anything else on your part: no religion, no chanting (unless you want to), and no special equipment. I wish you all good things as you start your exciting trip toward a better, more fulfilling life!

Introduction

So, you've decided to dive into the world of mindful meditation. That's awesome! But before we get started, let's take a moment to understand what mindful meditation is all about. Picture this: You're sitting quietly, focusing on your breath, and suddenly, your mind starts wandering off to that embarrassing moment from last week or your never-ending to-do list. Sound familiar? Well, that's where mindful meditation comes in!

Mindful meditation is like a superpower that helps you train your brain to stay in the present moment. It's not about emptying your mind or reaching some mystical state of enlightenment. Nope, it's simply about being aware of your thoughts, feelings, and surroundings without getting caught up in them. It's like having a front-row seat to your own mind and saying, "Hey, I see you, thought, but I'm just gonna sit here and breathe."

You see, our minds are constantly buzzing with activity. We're always thinking about the past, worrying about the future, or just getting lost in a sea of random thoughts. It's like having a monkey in your head jumping from one branch to another, never really settling down. And while this constant mental chatter can be entertaining at times, it can also be exhausting and stressful.

That's where mindful meditation comes in. By taking a few minutes each day to sit quietly and focus on your breath, you're giving your mind a much-needed break. You're training your brain to be more present, more aware, and more in control. It's like going to the gym for your mind!

But here's the thing: Mindful meditation isn't just some woo-woo practice reserved for yoga retreats and hippie communes. It's a scientifically proven technique that can have real, tangible benefits for your mental and physical health. Studies have shown that regular mindfulness practice can reduce stress, anxiety, and depression, improve focus and concentration, and even boost your immune system (Park et al., 2019). It's like a one-stop-shop for all your wellness needs!

And the best part? You don't need any fancy equipment or special skills to get started. All you need is a quiet space, a few minutes of your time, and a willingness to give it a try. Whether you're a busy professional, a stressed-out student, or just someone looking to find a little more peace in their life, mindful meditation can help.

Now, you might be thinking, *That's great, but how is this going to help me in my daily life?* Well, buckle up, because mindful meditation can be a game changer! By practicing regularly, you'll start to notice that you're less reactive to stress, more focused on the task at hand, and generally more chill. It's like having a secret weapon against the chaos of modern life.

Think about it: How often do you find yourself getting caught up in worry, anxiety, or self-doubt? How often do you feel like you're just going through the motions, not really present in your own life? Mindful meditation can help you break free from these patterns and cultivate a greater sense of clarity, purpose, and well-being.

But don't just take my word for it. Give it a try for yourself! Start with just a few minutes a day and see how it feels. You might be surprised at how quickly you start to notice a difference. And if you find it challenging at first, don't worry—that's totally normal. Like any new skill, mindfulness takes practice and patience. But with a little persistence, you'll start to see the benefits in no time.

In this book, we'll take you on a step-by-step journey through the world of mindful meditation. We'll start with the basics, like finding a comfortable position and focusing on your breath. Then, we'll explore more advanced techniques and ways to incorporate mindfulness into your daily routine. Whether you're a total beginner or have some experience with meditation, this book has got you covered.

We'll also dive into the science behind mindfulness, exploring how it affects the brain and body. You'll learn about the different types of meditation practices, from body scans to loving-kindness meditations, and discover which ones work best for you. And we'll tackle some of the common challenges and misconceptions about mindfulness so you can feel confident and empowered on your journey.

But perhaps most importantly, this book is about more than just meditation. It's about cultivating a mindful approach to life—one that allows you to be more present, more compassionate, and more in tune with yourself and others. By integrating mindfulness into your daily routine, you'll start to see the world in a new light. You'll be better equipped to handle stress, navigate relationships, and find a greater sense of meaning and purpose in your life.

Whether you're looking to reduce anxiety, improve your focus, or simply find a little more peace and happiness in your day-to-day life, this book is for you. It's a practical, accessible guide to mindfulness that will meet you where you're at and help you take your practice to the next level.

So, what are you waiting for? Grab a cushion, find a quiet spot, and let's get started on this mindfulness adventure together! Trust me, your brain (and probably everyone around you) will thank you. With a little practice and a lot of curiosity, you'll be well on your way to a more mindful, fulfilling life.

Chapter 1:

Understanding Mindful Meditation

Mindfulness is the practice of being fully present and aware in the current moment, without judgment. It's about tuning into your thoughts, feelings, and sensations and observing them with a sense of curiosity and acceptance. Think of it like taking a step back from the constant chatter in your mind and just being a neutral observer.

At its core, mindfulness is about paying attention. But it's a different kind of attention than what we're used to. In our fast-paced, multitasking world, we often find ourselves splitting our attention between multiple things at once, never fully engaging with any of them. Mindfulness, on the other hand, is about giving your full, undivided attention to the present moment.

This might sound simple, but it's actually a lot harder than it seems. Our minds are constantly wandering, jumping from thought to thought like a monkey swinging from branch to branch of a tree. We get caught up in worries about the future or regrets about the past and, before we know it, we've missed out on the richness of the present moment.

Mindfulness meditation is a way to train your brain to be more present and aware. By taking a few minutes each day to sit quietly and focus on your breath, you develop the skill of observing your thoughts and feelings without getting caught up in them. You learn to approach life with a greater sense of clarity and equanimity, even in the face of stress and challenges.

One of the key aspects of mindfulness is learning to cultivate a nonjudgmental attitude toward our experiences. This means observing our thoughts and feelings without labeling them as good or bad, right or wrong. Instead, we simply acknowledge them as they are, without getting caught up in the story they're telling.

This nonjudgmental awareness can be incredibly freeing. When we're able to observe our thoughts and feelings without getting swept away by them, we create a sense of space and perspective that allows us to respond to life's challenges with greater wisdom and compassion.

Another important aspect of mindfulness is learning to cultivate a sense of curiosity and openness toward our experiences. Rather than trying to push away difficult thoughts or feelings, we learn to approach them with a sense of interest and exploration. We might ask ourselves, "What is this thought or feeling trying to tell me? What can I learn from it?"

This curious, open attitude can help us develop a deeper understanding of ourselves and our place in the world. We might start to see patterns in our thoughts and behaviors that we hadn't noticed before and gain insight into what drives us and what holds us back.

Of course, cultivating mindfulness is easier said than done. It takes practice and patience to train our minds to be more present and aware. But the good news is that mindfulness is a skill that can be learned by anyone, regardless of age, background, or belief system.

One of the most accessible ways to practice mindfulness is through meditation. By setting aside a few minutes each day to sit quietly and focus on our breath, we can begin to develop the muscle of attention and awareness. Over time, this practice can spill over into other areas of our lives, helping us to be more present and engaged in everything we do.

But mindfulness isn't just about meditation. It's about bringing a sense of presence and awareness to all aspects of our lives, from the mundane tasks of daily living to the bigger questions of meaning and purpose. We can practice mindfulness while washing the dishes, walking in nature, or having a conversation with a friend. The key is to approach each moment with a sense of openness and curiosity, and to notice what arises without getting caught up in judgment or reactivity.

Brief History of Mindful Meditation

The practice of mindfulness meditation has a long and rich history, dating back thousands of years to ancient Buddhist traditions. In these traditions, meditation was seen as a powerful tool for cultivating wisdom, compassion, and inner peace. By training the mind to be more present and aware, practitioners believed they could gain insight into the nature of reality and experience a deeper sense of connection with all beings.

Despite its spiritual roots, mindfulness meditation is a secular practice that can be enjoyed by people of all beliefs and backgrounds. In the 1970s, a man named Jon Kabat-Zinn helped bring mindfulness into the mainstream through his groundbreaking work at the University of Massachusetts Medical Center.

Kabat-Zinn, a molecular biologist turned meditation teacher, developed a program called mindfulness-based stress reduction (MBSR) to help patients with chronic pain and stress-related conditions. The program was a huge success, and it quickly gained popularity among healthcare professionals and the general public alike.

Since then, mindfulness has exploded in popularity, with countless books, apps, and courses popping up to teach people how to meditate and live more mindfully. Today, mindfulness is used in a wide range of settings, from schools and workplaces to hospitals and therapy offices. It's even being studied by scientists around the world, who are uncovering more and more evidence of its powerful benefits for both mental and physical health.

One of the reasons mindfulness has become so popular in recent years is that it offers a simple, accessible way to cultivate greater well-being in our lives. Unlike some other forms of meditation or spiritual practice, mindfulness doesn't require any special equipment or training. All you need is a quiet space and a willingness to show up and pay attention.

Another reason mindfulness has gained traction is that it has been validated by science. Numerous studies have shown that regular mindfulness practice can lead to significant improvements in mental and physical health, from reduced stress and anxiety to improved immune function and chronic pain management (Park et al., 2019).

But perhaps the most compelling reason to practice mindfulness is the way it can transform our relationship with ourselves and the world around us. By learning to be more present and aware, we open ourselves up to a deeper sense of connection and meaning. We start to see the beauty and richness in the small moments of life, and we develop a greater capacity for compassion and understanding.

Benefits of Practicing Mindfulness

So, what exactly are these benefits? Let's take a closer look.

Reduced Stress and Anxiety

One of the most well-known benefits of mindfulness meditation is its ability to reduce stress and anxiety. When we're feeling overwhelmed or anxious, our minds tend to get caught up in negative thought patterns that only make things worse. We might worry about the future, replay past mistakes, or get caught in a spiral of self-criticism.

Mindfulness helps break this cycle by teaching us to observe our thoughts and feelings without getting caught up in them. By learning to step back and watch our mental chatter with a sense of curiosity and acceptance, we can start to see our thoughts for what they are: just thoughts, not necessarily reality.

This doesn't mean that mindfulness eliminates stress and anxiety altogether. Life will always have its challenges and difficult moments. But with a regular mindfulness practice, we can develop the resilience and inner strength to navigate these challenges with greater ease and equanimity.

Studies have shown that mindfulness meditation can be as effective as medication in treating anxiety and depression, without the side effects. It can also help us develop a greater sense of self-compassion and acceptance, which can be a powerful antidote to the self-criticism and negative self-talk that often fuel anxiety and stress (Keng et al., 2011).

Improved Focus and Concentration

In addition to reducing stress and anxiety, mindfulness has been shown to improve focus and concentration. In our multitasking world, it's easy to get distracted and lose sight of what's important. We might find ourselves jumping from task to task, never fully engaging with any of them.

Mindfulness helps train our attention by teaching us to focus on one thing at a time, whether it's our breath, a sensation in our body, or a task at hand. With practice, we can develop the ability to sustain our attention for longer periods of time, even in the face of distractions and interruptions.

This improved focus and concentration can have a ripple effect throughout our lives. We might find ourselves being more productive at work, more engaged in our hobbies and relationships, and more able to pursue our goals and dreams with clarity and purpose.

Studies have shown that regular mindfulness practice can actually change the structure and function of our brains, increasing the density of gray matter in areas associated with attention, learning, and memory (Hölzel et al. 2011). It can also help us develop greater cognitive flexibility, allowing us to switch between tasks more easily and adapt to changing circumstances.

Enhanced Emotional Regulation

Another key benefit of mindfulness is its ability to enhance emotional regulation. When we're caught up in strong emotions like anger, sadness, or fear, it can be hard to think clearly or make good decisions.

We might lash out at others, withdraw from social situations, or engage in self-destructive behaviors.

Mindfulness helps us develop a healthier relationship with our emotions by teaching us to observe them without judgment. Instead of getting swept away by our feelings, we can learn to step back and see them for what they are—temporary experiences that come and go like waves on the ocean.

With practice, we can start to develop a greater sense of emotional balance and resilience. We might find ourselves being less reactive to difficult situations, more able to communicate our needs and boundaries, and more compassionate toward ourselves and others.

Research has shown that mindfulness can be particularly helpful for people struggling with emotional disorders like depression, anxiety, and PTSD (Keng et al, 2011). By learning to observe and accept their emotions without judgment, they can start to develop a greater sense of self-awareness and self-compassion, which can be a powerful tool for healing and growth.

Improved Physical Health

In addition to its mental and emotional benefits, mindfulness has been shown to have a positive impact on physical health as well. Research suggests that regular mindfulness practice can lower blood pressure, improve immune function, and even reduce chronic pain (Keng et al, 2011).

One reason for this is that mindfulness helps reduce stress, which is known to have a negative impact on physical health. When we're stressed, our bodies release hormones like cortisol and adrenaline, which can lead to inflammation, weakened immunity, and other health problems over time.

By reducing stress and promoting relaxation, mindfulness can help mitigate these negative effects and support overall physical well-being. It can also help us develop greater awareness of our bodies and their needs, such as the importance of proper nutrition, exercise, and sleep.

Studies have shown that mindfulness can be particularly helpful for people with chronic health conditions like heart disease, diabetes, and fibromyalgia (Keng et al, 2011). By learning to tune into their bodies and respond to their needs with greater care and compassion, they can often manage their symptoms more effectively and improve their overall quality of life.

Increased Self-Awareness and Insight

Perhaps one of the most profound benefits of mindfulness is its ability to increase self-awareness and insight. When we're caught up in the busyness of daily life, it's easy to lose touch with ourselves and our deepest values and aspirations.

Mindfulness helps us cultivate a deeper understanding of ourselves by teaching us to observe our thoughts, feelings, and behaviors with curiosity and acceptance. We might start to notice patterns or habits that we weren't aware of before, such as a tendency to procrastinate or a fear of failure.

With this increased self-awareness comes the opportunity for greater insight and personal growth. We might start to see our lives in a new light, with a greater sense of clarity and purpose. We might also develop a deeper sense of compassion and understanding for ourselves and others, recognizing that we are all works in progress, doing the best we can with what we have.

Research has shown that mindfulness can be a powerful tool for self-discovery and personal transformation (Phang & Oei, 2012). By learning to observe our thoughts and feelings with greater awareness and acceptance, we can start to identify the beliefs and patterns that hold us back and develop new ways of thinking and being that are more aligned with our values and goals.

Improved Relationships and Communication

Another often-overlooked benefit of mindfulness is its ability to improve our relationships and communication with others. When we're more present and aware in our interactions, we're better able to listen deeply, express ourselves clearly, and respond with empathy and compassion.

Mindfulness can help us develop greater emotional intelligence, allowing us to pick up on subtle cues and respond to others' needs with greater sensitivity and skill. It can also help us communicate more effectively by teaching us to speak from a place of clarity and intention rather than reactivity or defensiveness.

Studies have shown that couples who practice mindfulness together report greater relationship satisfaction, better communication, and increased feelings of closeness and intimacy (Kappen et al., 2018). Mindfulness can also be helpful in the workplace, by promoting greater collaboration, creativity, and conflict resolution among team members.

Greater Sense of Purpose and Meaning

Finally, mindfulness can help us cultivate a greater sense of purpose and meaning in our lives. By learning to be more present and aware, we open ourselves up to the richness and beauty of each moment and start to see the interconnectedness of all things.

Mindfulness can help us develop a deeper sense of gratitude and appreciation for the simple joys of life, from the warmth of the sun on our skin to the laughter of a child. It can also help us connect with our deepest values and aspirations and align our actions with what truly matters to us.

Studies have shown that people who practice mindfulness regularly report greater feelings of purpose, meaning, and life satisfaction (Keng et al., 2011). They also tend to be more engaged in their communities and more committed to making a positive difference in the world.

Mindfulness meditation is a powerful tool for cultivating greater presence, awareness, and well-being in our lives. By learning to observe our thoughts and feelings with curiosity and acceptance, we can develop the resilience and inner strength to navigate life's challenges with greater ease and equanimity.

Whether you're looking to reduce stress and anxiety, improve focus and concentration, or simply develop a deeper understanding of yourself and your place in the world, mindfulness has something to offer. With practice and patience, you too can experience the many benefits of this ancient practice in your own life.

Exercise: Mindful Breathing

Find a quiet and comfortable space where you can sit without distractions. Sit in a relaxed, upright position, either on a cushion or on a chair. Allow your eyes to gently close, or maintain a soft gaze toward the ground.

Bring your attention to your breath. Notice the sensation of the air moving in and out of your nostrils, the gentle rise and fall of your chest, and the movement of your belly. Observe the breath without trying to control or change it; simply let it flow naturally.

As you continue to focus on your breath, you may notice your mind starting to wander. This is completely normal and happens to everyone. When you catch your mind drifting off, gently acknowledge the thoughts or distractions and then redirect your attention back to your breath.

If you find your mind getting caught up in a particular thought or emotion, try labeling it silently in your mind. For example, if you notice yourself thinking about your to-do list, silently say "thinking" and then return your focus to your breath. If you notice a feeling of anxiety arising, silently say "feeling" and then come back to your breath.

Remember, the goal isn't to stop your thoughts or achieve a blank state of mind. The aim is to build your capacity to observe your thoughts and emotions without getting caught up in them, and to gently redirect your attention back to the present moment.

Start with just five minutes of mindful breathing and gradually increase the duration over time. You might set a timer or use a guided meditation app to help you stay on track.

As you continue to practice mindful breathing, you may start to notice subtle changes in your state of mind. You may feel a bit more centered, grounded, and present. You may find it easier to let go of stressful thoughts and emotions.

Over time, the practice of mindful breathing can help you cultivate a greater sense of awareness, calm, and resilience in your daily life. It's a simple yet powerful tool that you can use anytime, anywhere, to reconnect with the present moment and find a sense of inner peace and clarity.

Remember, mindfulness is a practice, not a perfect. Be patient and kind with yourself as you explore this new way of being. Trust that each moment of awareness is planting a seed that will blossom in its own time.

Chapter 2:

Getting Started

Alright, so you're ready to dive into the wonderful world of mindfulness meditation. You've heard about all the amazing benefits, from reducing stress and anxiety to improving focus and overall well-being, and you're eager to experience them for yourself. But where do you even begin? Don't worry, we've got you covered!

In this chapter, we'll explore the essential steps for getting started with your mindfulness practice. We'll talk about creating a sacred space for meditation, finding the right posture, and setting realistic expectations. By the end of this chapter, you'll have all the tools you need to start your mindfulness journey with confidence and ease.

Creating a Sacred Space for Meditation

First things first: Let's talk about creating a sacred space for your meditation practice. Now, when I say "sacred space," I don't mean you need to build a fancy altar or burn incense or anything like that (although if that's your thing, go for it!). What I mean is simply finding a quiet, comfortable place where you can sit and be with yourself without distractions.

This might be a corner of your bedroom, a spot in your backyard, or even a quiet room at your workplace. The key is to find a place that feels safe, peaceful, and conducive to turning inward. If possible, try to choose a spot that you can use consistently for your practice, as this will help create a sense of ritual and familiarity over time.

Once you've chosen your spot, take a few moments to make it feel special. You might light a candle, place a favorite object nearby, or simply take a few deep breaths to clear the energy of the space. The idea is to create a sense of intention and sacredness around your practice so that when you sit down to meditate, you feel like you're entering a special time and place.

Of course, life being what it is, there will be times when you can't access your sacred space. Maybe you're traveling, or you have kids or roommates who make it impossible to find a quiet moment alone. In these cases, don't worry! Remember, the most important sacred space is the one within yourself. As long as you can find a few moments of quiet and stillness, you can meditate anywhere, anytime.

When creating your sacred space, it's also important to consider the environment around you. Is the lighting soft and calming or harsh and distracting? Is the temperature comfortable or too hot or cold? Are there any sounds or smells that might pull you out of your practice?

Take some time to experiment with different environmental factors until you find what works best for you. Maybe you prefer complete silence, or maybe you find that a little background noise actually helps you focus. Maybe you like to meditate in a cool, dark room, or maybe you prefer a warm, sunlit space. There's no right or wrong answer here—the key is to find what feels most supportive and nourishing for your practice.

Another thing to consider when creating your sacred space is the energy you bring to it. Before you sit down to meditate, take a moment to check in with yourself. How are you feeling, physically and emotionally? Are you carrying any tension or stress in your body? Are there any thoughts or worries weighing on your mind?

Rather than trying to push these things away, see if you can simply acknowledge them with kindness and compassion. Take a few deep breaths and imagine yourself releasing any tension or stress with each exhalation. Set an intention for your practice, whether it's to find a sense of calm, to cultivate self-awareness, or simply to be present with whatever arises.

By bringing a sense of intention and care to your sacred space, you'll create a supportive environment for your practice to unfold. And remember, your sacred space doesn't have to be perfect; it just has to be yours. With time and consistency, you'll start to associate this space with a sense of peace, clarity, and connection to yourself.

Finding the Right Posture

Now that you've created your sacred space, it's time to talk about posture. When most people think of meditation, they picture someone sitting cross-legged on a cushion, eyes closed, hands resting on their knees. And while this is certainly one way to meditate, it's not the only way!

The truth is, there's no one "right" posture for meditation. The most important thing is to find a position that allows you to be comfortable and alert at the same time. This might mean sitting on a cushion or a chair, or even lying down (although be careful with lying down, as it's easy to fall asleep!).

If you do choose to sit, there are a few things to keep in mind. First, try to sit with your back straight but not rigid. Imagine a string pulling you up from the crown of your head, elongating your spine and creating a sense of spaciousness in your torso. This will help you stay alert and focused during your practice.

Next, make sure your hips are higher than your knees. This will help keep your spine straight and prevent your legs from falling asleep. If you're sitting on a cushion, you might try folding a blanket or towel under your hips to elevate them slightly. If you're sitting in a chair, make sure your feet are flat on the ground and your back is supported.

Finally, rest your hands on your thighs or lap and find a comfortable position for your head and neck. You might try closing your eyes, or keeping them slightly open and gazing downward. The key is to find a position that feels natural and easy to maintain for the duration of your practice.

Remember, it's okay if your posture isn't perfect at first. Like anything else, it takes practice to find a position that feels comfortable and sustainable. Be patient with yourself, and don't be afraid to experiment until you find what works for you.

One thing to keep in mind is that your posture may change over time as your practice deepens. What feels comfortable in the beginning may not feel as comfortable after a few weeks or months of consistent practice. This is totally normal, and it's a sign that your body is adapting to the practice.

If you find that your posture is causing you pain or discomfort, don't hesitate to adjust or try something new. You might experiment with different cushions or supports or try sitting in a different position altogether. The goal is to find a posture that allows you to be present and focused without causing undue strain or tension in your body.

Another thing to consider is the length of your practice. When you're first starting out, it's okay to keep your sessions short—even just a few minutes at a time. As you build up your endurance and comfort with the practice, you can gradually increase the length of your sessions.

But even as you practice for longer periods of time, remember to listen to your body and take breaks when you need them. If you find yourself getting fidgety or uncomfortable, it's okay to stand up, stretch, or take a few deep breaths before settling back into your posture.

Ultimately, the key to finding the right posture is to approach it with a sense of curiosity and experimentation. Don't be afraid to try new things, and don't get too attached to any one way of sitting or being. With time and practice, you'll find a posture that feels natural, comfortable, and supportive of your mindfulness practice.

Setting Realistic Expectations

Okay, so you've created your sacred space and found your perfect posture. You're ready to start meditating and experience all those amazing benefits you've heard about. But before you dive in, let's talk about setting realistic expectations.

Here's the thing: Mindfulness meditation is not a quick fix or a magic bullet. It's not going to solve all your problems overnight, and it's not going to turn you into a zen master after just a few sessions. Like any skill, mindfulness takes time, patience, and practice to develop.

When you first start meditating, you might find that your mind is constantly wandering, jumping from thought to thought like a monkey in a tree. This is totally normal! In fact, it's the whole point of mindfulness meditation: to notice when your mind has wandered and gently bring it back to the present moment.

So, don't beat yourself up if you find it hard to focus at first. Don't worry if you feel like you're "doing it wrong" or "not getting it." These are all common experiences for beginning meditators, and they don't mean you're failing at mindfulness. They simply mean you're human, with a human mind that likes to wander and get distracted.

The key is to approach your practice with a sense of curiosity and a lack of judgment. When you notice your mind has wandered, simply acknowledge it without getting frustrated or discouraged. Gently bring your attention back to your breath, or whatever anchor you're using for your practice. And if your mind wanders again (which it will), simply repeat the process.

Over time, with consistent practice, you'll start to notice that your mind wanders less often and that you're able to bring it back more quickly and easily. You might also start to notice subtle changes in your daily life, like feeling less reactive to stress or more present in your interactions with others.

But these changes happen gradually, and they're not always easy to see at first. So, it's important to approach your practice with patience and self-compassion. Remember, mindfulness is a journey, not a destination. There's no end point or finish line to cross. The goal is simply to show up, day after day, and be present with whatever arises.

So, start small and be realistic in your expectations. Aim for just a few minutes of practice each day and gradually build up over time. And if you miss a day (or two, or ten), don't worry! Just start again the next day, without judgment or self-criticism.

Remember, the most important thing is to approach your practice with an open and curious mind. Don't put too much pressure on yourself to "get it right" or achieve some kind of perfect state of mindfulness. Simply show up, be present, and let the practice unfold in its own time.

It's also important to remember that mindfulness is not a one-size-fits-all practice. What works for one person may not work for another, and that's okay. Some people find that they prefer guided meditations, while others prefer silent practice. Some people like to meditate in the morning, while others find that evening works better for them.

The key is to experiment and find what works best for you. Don't be afraid to try different techniques, teachers, or styles of practice until you find something that resonates with you. And remember, your practice will likely evolve over time as you deepen your understanding and experience of mindfulness.

Another thing to keep in mind is that mindfulness is not just about meditation. While a formal meditation practice is certainly an important part of developing mindfulness, it's not the only way to cultivate present-moment awareness. You can bring mindfulness to any activity, from cooking and eating to walking and talking. Simply by paying attention to your senses and your experience in the present moment, you can start to cultivate a greater sense of presence and awareness in your daily life.

So, don't feel like you have to limit your practice to the cushion. Look for opportunities to bring mindfulness into your everyday activities, whether it's savoring your morning coffee or taking a few deep breaths before a stressful meeting. Over time, you'll start to develop a more continuous sense of mindfulness that permeates your entire life.

Exercise: Creating a Mindfulness Corner

One of the keys to establishing a consistent mindfulness practice is to create a dedicated space that supports your intention to be present and aware. This exercise invites you to create a mindfulness corner in your home or office, which will be a special place that you can return to each day to nurture your practice.

Start by choosing a quiet, comfortable spot where you can sit without distractions. This might be a corner of your bedroom, a peaceful spot in your living room, or even a quiet area in your office.

Once you've selected your space, take some time to clear away any clutter or distractions. You want this to be a place of simplicity and calm, free from the usual stressors and stimuli of daily life.

Next, gather a few key items to include in your mindfulness corner. A comfortable cushion or chair is essential, as you'll want to be able to sit with ease and stability. You might also include a small table or altar where you can place meaningful objects or symbols of your practice.

Consider adding a few natural elements to your space, such as a plant, a vase of flowers, or a bowl of stones. These can help to create a sense of groundedness and connection to the natural world.

If you find inspiration in certain texts or teachings, you might include a few books or quotes that resonate with you. You could also add a journal and pen for reflecting on your practice.

Finally, consider including any other objects or elements that help to create a sense of sacredness and intention in your space. This might be a candle, a piece of artwork, or a special photo or memento.

Once you've created your mindfulness corner, commit to spending a few minutes there each day. You might sit for a formal meditation practice, do a few mindful stretches, or simply take a few deep breaths and set an intention for your day.

Over time, your mindfulness corner will become a sacred space that supports and sustains your practice. It will be a place of refuge and renewal, a reminder to pause and reconnect with what matters most.

As you continue to return to your mindfulness corner each day, notice how it feels to have this dedicated space in your life. Notice any shifts in your energy, your focus, or your overall sense of well-being.

Remember, your mindfulness corner doesn't have to be perfect or elaborate. The most important thing is that it feels authentic and nourishing to you. Trust your own intuition and let your space evolve over time as your practice deepens and grows.

Chapter 3:

The Basics of Mindful Meditation

Congratulations! You've created your sacred space, found your perfect posture, and set some realistic expectations for your mindfulness practice. You're officially ready to dive into the nuts and bolts of mindful meditation. But wait, what exactly does that entail? And how do you know if you're doing it "right"? Don't worry, we'll cover all of that and more in this chapter.

Breath Awareness Meditation

First up, let's talk about one of the most fundamental techniques in mindfulness meditation: breath awareness. This simple yet powerful practice involves focusing your attention on the sensations of breathing, and using your breath as an anchor to bring you back to the present moment whenever your mind starts to wander.

To try it out, find a comfortable seated position (remember what we talked about in the last chapter!) and gently close your eyes. Take a few deep breaths, feeling the air moving in and out of your lungs. Then let your breath settle into its natural rhythm, without trying to control or change it in any way.

Now, bring your attention to the sensation of the breath moving through your nostrils. Notice the feeling of the cool air entering your nose on the inhale and the warm air leaving your nose on the exhale. You might also notice the gentle rise and fall of your chest or belly as you breathe.

As you focus on these sensations, you'll probably notice that your mind starts to wander. Maybe you start thinking about your to-do list, or that conversation you had with your boss yesterday, or what you're going to have for dinner tonight. This is totally normal! The mind's job is to think, and it's not going to stop just because you've decided to meditate.

The key is to notice when your mind has wandered and gently bring your attention back to your breath. You might even try silently noting "thinking" or "wandering" when you catch your mind drifting; this will allow you to acknowledge the thought without getting caught up in it.

And if you find yourself getting frustrated or discouraged when your mind wanders (which it will, a lot), remember to be kind and patient with yourself. This is a practice, not a performance. The goal is not to stop your mind from thinking altogether, but rather to cultivate a new relationship with your thoughts: one that is more spacious, curious, and compassionate.

So, keep coming back to your breath, again and again, without judgment or expectation. Over time, you'll start to develop a deeper sense of presence and awareness, both on and off the cushion.

Body Scan Meditation

Another powerful technique in mindfulness meditation is the body scan. This practice involves systematically directing your attention to different parts of your body, from the top of your head to the tips of your toes, and noticing any sensations that arise along the way.

To try it out, lie down on your back in a comfortable position, with your arms at your sides and your feet falling away from each other. Take a few deep breaths, then bring your attention to the top of your head.

Notice any sensations in this area, such as tingling, pulsing, or pressure. You might also notice temperature, such as warmth or coolness. Whatever you feel, just notice it without trying to change or judge it.

After a few moments, let your attention move down to your face, noticing any sensations in your forehead, eyes, cheeks, nose, and mouth. Then, move your attention down to your neck and shoulders, noticing any tension or tightness in these areas.

Continue moving your attention down your body, spending a few moments with each part: your arms, hands, chest, belly, hips, legs, and feet. Notice any sensations that arise, whether pleasant, unpleasant, or neutral. If your mind starts to wander, gently bring it back to the part of the body you were focusing on.

When you've scanned your entire body, take a few deep breaths and notice how you feel. You might feel more relaxed, more present, or more in tune with your physical experience. You might also notice areas of tension or discomfort that you weren't aware of before.

The body scan is a powerful way to cultivate mindfulness because it helps you connect with your physical experience in a more direct and intimate way. By bringing your attention to your body, you can start to notice patterns of tension, stress, or holding that you might not be aware of otherwise.

And, like breath awareness, the body scan is a practice that you can come back to again and again, deepening your awareness and presence each time.

Mindfulness of Thoughts and Emotions

So far, we've talked about using the breath and the body as anchors for our mindfulness practice. But what about those pesky thoughts and emotions that keep pulling us out of the present moment? Can we be mindful of those too?

Absolutely! In fact, learning to be mindful of our thoughts and emotions is a crucial part of the practice. When we're caught up in our mental chatter or swept away by strong emotions, it can be hard to find our way back to the present moment. But by learning to observe our thoughts and emotions with curiosity and kindness, we can start to create a little more space and freedom in our lives.

One way to practice mindfulness of thoughts is to imagine them as clouds passing through the sky. When a thought arises, whether it's a worry, a memory, or a plan for the future, see if you can simply notice it without getting caught up in the content. You might even try labeling the thought as "thinking," as a way of acknowledging it without identifying with it.

Another way to practice mindfulness of thoughts is to notice the patterns and themes that arise in your mental chatter. Do you tend to worry about the future or ruminate on the past? Do you have a harsh inner critic or a tendency to compare yourself to others? By becoming more aware of these patterns, you can start to develop a more balanced and compassionate relationship with your thoughts.

When it comes to emotions, mindfulness can be a powerful tool for navigating the ups and downs of your inner world. When a strong emotion arises, whether it's anger, sadness, or joy, see if you can simply be present with it, without trying to push it away or hold onto it.

You might try naming the emotion, such as "anger" or "sadness," as a way of acknowledging it without getting lost in the story behind it. You might also notice how the emotion feels in your body, such as a tightness in your chest or a warmth in your belly.

By learning to be present with your emotions, you can start to develop a greater sense of equanimity and resilience. You will learn that emotions are temporary, changeable experiences, and that you can be with them without being overwhelmed by them.

Of course, this is easier said than done, especially when it comes to difficult or painful emotions. It's important to remember that mindfulness is not about suppressing or ignoring your emotions, but rather about learning to relate to them with greater awareness and compassion.

If you find yourself struggling with intense or overwhelming emotions, it may be helpful to seek the support of a therapist or counselor who can help you develop additional coping strategies.

Integrating Mindfulness Into Daily Life

As we've seen, mindfulness meditation can be a powerful tool for cultivating greater awareness, presence, and well-being in our lives. But the practice doesn't have to stop when we leave the cushion. In fact, one of the greatest benefits of mindfulness is the way it can infuse our daily lives with greater presence and purpose.

One way to bring mindfulness into your daily life is to choose a few simple activities that you do every day and make them into mindfulness practices. For example, you might try bringing mindfulness to your morning coffee ritual by noticing the warmth of the mug in your hands, the aroma of the coffee, and the taste and texture of each sip.

Or you might try bringing mindfulness to your daily commute by noticing the sensation of your feet on the ground, the sounds and sights around you, and the feeling of the air on your skin.

The key is to approach these activities with the same sense of curiosity and presence that you bring to your formal meditation practice. By infusing your daily life with mindfulness, you can start to create a more continuous sense of awareness and connection, even in the midst of your busy, fast-paced world.

Another way to integrate mindfulness into your daily life is to practice mindful communication. This means bringing a sense of presence and care to your interactions with others, whether it's with your partner, your kids, your colleagues, or the barista at your local coffee shop.

When you're in conversation with someone, see if you can give them your full attention, without getting distracted by your phone or your own mental chatter. Notice the tone of their voice, the expression on their face, and the words they're using. See if you can listen with an open and curious mind, without jumping to conclusions or judgments.

And when it's your turn to speak, see if you can do so with clarity and kindness, choosing your words carefully and speaking from a place of authenticity and care.

By bringing mindfulness to your communication, you can start to build deeper, more meaningful relationships with the people in your life. You will learn to listen more deeply, speak more truthfully, and connect more authentically with others.

Of course, like any practice, integrating mindfulness into your daily life takes time and patience. It's not about perfection, but rather about showing up with presence and care, moment by moment, day by day.

And as you continue to practice, both on and off the cushion, you may start to notice subtle shifts in the way you relate to yourself, others, and the world around you. You may find that you're a little less reactive, a little more compassionate, and a little more attuned to the beauty and mystery of each moment.

Chapter 4:

Building a Consistent Practice

By now, you've learned the basics of mindful meditation, from breath awareness and body scans to mindfulness of thoughts and emotions. You've even started to explore how to integrate these practices into your daily life, infusing your ordinary moments with greater presence and purpose.

But here's the thing: Mindfulness isn't a one-and-done kind of deal. It's not something you can master in a weekend workshop or a 10-day retreat, then call it a day. To truly reap the benefits of mindfulness, you need to make it a consistent, ongoing practice and a regular part of your daily routine, like brushing your teeth or getting dressed in the morning.

Now, I know what you might be thinking: *But I'm so busy! I barely have time to eat breakfast, let alone sit in silence for 30 minutes a day. And even when I do find the time to meditate, my mind is so restless, I can barely sit still for five minutes without fidgeting or falling asleep!*

Trust me, I get it. Building a consistent mindfulness practice can be challenging, especially in our fast-paced, distraction-filled world. But with a little patience, persistence, and a healthy dose of self-compassion, it's totally doable—and so, so worth it.

In this chapter, we'll explore some practical strategies for establishing a daily meditation routine, gradually increasing the duration of your sessions, and dealing with common challenges like restlessness and sleepiness. We'll also talk about how to transition from guided to self-guided meditation, track your progress and set goals, and bridge the gap between formal practice and informal mindfulness moments.

Establishing a Daily Meditation Routine

First things first: If you want to make mindfulness a consistent practice, you need to carve out some dedicated time for it in your daily schedule. And I'm not talking about squeezing in a quick five-minute session between meetings or scrolling through your phone. I'm talking about setting aside a specific, non-negotiable chunk of time each day to sit in silence and cultivate your awareness.

Now, I know this can feel daunting, especially if you're already feeling overwhelmed or stretched thin. But here's the thing: You don't need to start with a 30-minute or even a 20-minute session right off the bat. In fact, I'd recommend starting with just five or ten minutes a day and gradually building up from there.

The key is to pick a time that works for you, and then stick to it as best you can. For some people, first thing in the morning works best, before the demands of the day have a chance to take over. For others, a midday break or an evening wind-down session feels more doable. There's no right or wrong answer here—the most important thing is to find a time that you can realistically commit to, day after day.

Once you've picked your time, try to create a dedicated space for your practice; this should be a quiet, comfortable spot where you can sit without too many distractions. It doesn't have to be a fancy meditation room or a serene outdoor oasis (although if you have access to those things, by all means, use them!). It can be as simple as a corner of your bedroom, a spot on your living room floor, or even a chair in your office.

The key is to make this space feel special and sacred—a place where you can let go of your daily concerns and connect with your inner world. You might add a few simple touches to make it feel more inviting, like a cozy cushion or blanket, a small plant or candle, or a meaningful object or image that inspires you.

Once you've got your time and space set up, try to approach your practice with a sense of curiosity and openness. Remember, the goal isn't to achieve some blissed-out state of perfect calm (although that can certainly happen from time to time). The goal is simply to show up, day after day, and observe your experience with kindness and acceptance, whatever that experience happens to be.

Gradually Increasing the Duration of Your Sessions

Okay, so you've established a daily meditation routine—congrats! That's a huge step in itself. But now you might be wondering how to build on that foundation and deepen your practice over time.

One way to do this is by gradually increasing the duration of your meditation sessions. Like I mentioned before, it's totally fine to start with just five or ten minutes a day; in fact, I'd recommend it. Trying to sit for too long too soon can be overwhelming and counterproductive, leading to frustration, restlessness, and even giving up altogether.

But as you start to get more comfortable with the practice, you might naturally find yourself wanting to sit for longer periods of time. And that's great! Just be sure to increase your session duration gradually, in small increments.

For example, let's say you've been sitting for five minutes a day for a week or two, and it's starting to feel pretty doable. You might try bumping it up to seven or eight minutes for the next week, then ten minutes the week after that. Or, if you're starting with 10 minutes, you might increase to 12 or 15 minutes, then 20, and so on.

The key is to listen to your own inner wisdom and not push yourself too hard or too fast. Some days, you might feel like you could sit for an hour without batting an eye. Other days, just making it to the cushion for five minutes might feel like a Herculean effort. And that's okay; it's all part of the practice.

Remember, the goal isn't to rack up meditation minutes like frequent flyer miles. The goal is to cultivate a sense of ease, curiosity, and self-compassion in your practice, and to let it unfold at its own natural pace.

Dealing With Common Challenges

Of course, even with the best of intentions and the most gradual of increases, building a consistent meditation practice is rarely a smooth, linear process. Sooner or later, you're bound to run into some common challenges: things like restlessness, sleepiness, boredom, doubt, and good old-fashioned resistance.

First of all, know that these experiences are totally normal and natural. In fact, they're an essential part of the practice. Mindfulness isn't about eliminating difficult thoughts or feelings; it's about learning to relate to them with greater awareness and acceptance.

That said, there are some practical strategies you can use to work with these challenges when they arise. Let's take a closer look at a few of the most common ones.

Restlessness

If you find yourself feeling fidgety, antsy, or like you just can't sit still, try bringing your attention to the physical sensations of restlessness in your body. Where do you feel it most strongly? What does it feel like— a buzzing, a tingling, a tightness? See if you can observe these sensations with curiosity and acceptance, without trying to change them or make them go away.

You might also try experimenting with your posture or your breathing. Sometimes, simply taking a few deep, slow breaths or adjusting your sitting position can help to settle both your body and mind.

Sleepiness

If you find yourself feeling drowsy or nodding off during your practice, first of all, don't beat yourself up about it. It's totally normal to feel a little sleepy, especially if you're new to meditation or practicing at a time of day when you're naturally more tired.

That said, if sleepiness is a consistent issue for you, there are a few things you can try. First, make sure you're getting enough sleep at night, and try to practice at a time of day when you're naturally more alert (like first thing in the morning or after exercising).

You might also try sitting up a bit straighter, taking a few deep breaths, or even opening your eyes slightly if you're practicing with them closed. And if you do find yourself drifting off, simply notice it with kindness and gently bring your attention back to your anchor (like your breath or your bodily sensations).

Boredom

If you find yourself feeling bored or disengaged during your practice, first of all, congratulations—you're human! Boredom is a totally natural response to sitting still and doing "nothing" for extended periods of time, especially in our fast-paced, stimulation-rich world.

When boredom arises, see if you can get curious about it. What does it feel like in your body? What thoughts or stories is your mind telling you about it? Can you observe these experiences with a sense of interest and acceptance without getting too caught up in them?

You might also try bringing a sense of fresh attention to your anchor, as if you're noticing it for the very first time. See if you can discover something new or surprising about the sensation of breathing or the feeling of your body making contact with the ground.

Doubt

If you find yourself feeling doubtful or skeptical about your meditation practice, wondering if it's really "working" or if you're doing it "right," know that this is a totally normal part of the journey. In fact, a healthy dose of doubt can actually be a sign of progress, as it means you're starting to question your assumptions and beliefs and opening up to new ways of seeing and being.

When doubt arises, see if you can meet it with curiosity and openness rather than trying to push it away or convince yourself otherwise. You might silently acknowledge it, saying to yourself something like, "Ah, doubt is here," and then gently bring your attention back to your present-moment experience.

You might also reflect on your intentions for practicing: Why did you start meditating in the first place? What benefits have you noticed so far, even if they're small or subtle? Can you connect with a sense of trust and faith in the practice, even in the face of uncertainty?

Resistance

Finally, if you find yourself feeling resistant or avoidant around your practice, like you just don't want to do it or you keep finding excuses not to, know that this is super common and totally understandable. In fact, resistance is often a sign that you're bumping up against something important—some deeper fear, belief, or pattern that's ready to be explored and transformed.

When resistance arises, see if you can meet it with compassion and understanding rather than judgment or self-criticism. Acknowledge that it's there, and see if you can get curious about what it might be trying to tell you.

You might also try setting some gentle, achievable goals for your practice and celebrating your small successes along the way. Maybe you could commit to meditating for just one minute a day for a week or reward yourself with a nice cup of tea after each session. The key is to find ways to make the practice feel more inviting and rewarding instead of it feeling like a chore or a punishment.

Transitioning From Guided to Self-Guided Meditation

As you continue to build your daily practice, you might find yourself starting to outgrow guided meditations and yearning for a bit more independence and autonomy in your sessions. And that's great! Guided meditations can be incredibly helpful for getting started and learning the basic techniques, but at some point, you might naturally want to spread your wings and fly solo.

If you're feeling ready to transition from guided to self-guided meditation, here are a few tips to keep in mind:

- **Start small:** Just like with increasing your session duration, it's best to make this transition gradually. You might start by doing a few minutes of self-guided practice at the end of a guided session, or try alternating between guided and self-guided sessions throughout the week.

- **Keep it simple:** When you're first starting out with self-guided practice, it's best to keep your technique simple and straightforward. Stick with a basic anchor, like your breath or bodily sensations, and just focus on observing your experience with curiosity and acceptance.

- **Be your own guide:** One of the benefits of self-guided meditation is that you get to be your own teacher and guide. You can experiment with different techniques and approaches and find what works best for you. Just remember to approach your practice with kindness and patience, and to trust your own inner wisdom.

- **Have a plan:** It can be helpful to have a rough outline or plan for your self-guided sessions, especially in the beginning. You might decide to focus on a particular theme or quality (like gratitude, compassion, or equanimity) or to structure your session around a specific technique (like a body scan or loving-kindness meditation).

- **Be open to change:** As you continue to practice self-guided meditation, be open to letting your sessions evolve and change over time. You might find that certain techniques or approaches that once worked well for you no longer feel as resonant, or that your practice naturally starts to take on a different flavor or focus. Trust the process, and be willing to adapt and adjust as needed.

Tracking Progress and Setting Goals

One of the keys to building a consistent, sustainable meditation practice is to find ways to stay motivated and engaged over the long haul. And one powerful way to do this is by tracking your progress and setting goals for your practice.

Now, I know the idea of "goals" and "progress" might sound a little antithetical to the spirit of mindfulness—after all, isn't the whole point to let go of striving and just be present with what is? And yes, that's absolutely true. But setting an intention and reflecting on your journey can also be a valuable way to deepen your commitment and cultivate a sense of purpose and direction in your practice.

The key is to approach goal-setting and tracking with a sense of curiosity and openness, rather than judgment or attachment. Here are a few tips to keep in mind:

- **Keep it simple:** Your goals don't have to be grand or elaborate; in fact, the simpler and more achievable, the better. You might set a goal to meditate for five minutes a day for a week, or to practice loving-kindness meditation once a week for a month. The key is to choose goals that feel inspiring and doable rather than overwhelming or burdensome.

- **Focus on the process, not the outcome:** Remember, the goal of mindfulness isn't to achieve some particular state or outcome (like perfect calm or endless bliss), but rather to cultivate a way of being that's more present, curious, and compassionate. So, instead of setting goals around specific results or experiences, focus on the qualities and intentions you want to bring to your practice.

- **Celebrate your successes:** When you do achieve a goal or milestone in your practice, take a moment to acknowledge and celebrate it! This doesn't have to be a big, flashy celebration—it can be as simple as taking a few deep breaths and silently congratulating yourself, or sharing your success with a supportive friend or community. The key is to reinforce the positive habit and give yourself a little boost of motivation and encouragement.

- **Be kind to yourself:** Of course, there will inevitably be times when you don't meet your goals or live up to your own expectations, and that's okay. When this happens, try to meet yourself with kindness and understanding rather than judgment or self-criticism. Remember, the practice of mindfulness is all about cultivating self-compassion and acceptance, even (and especially) in the face of challenges and setbacks.

As for tracking your progress, there are lots of different ways you can do this, from keeping a simple meditation journal to using a smartphone app or spreadsheet. The key is to find a method that feels easy and intuitive for you, and that helps you stay accountable and motivated without feeling like a burden or a chore.

You might track things like the date and duration of your sessions, any particular techniques or themes you focused on, and any insights, challenges, or successes you noticed along the way. Over time, this kind of tracking can help you identify patterns and trends in your practice, give you a sense of how far you've come, and decide where you might want to go next.

Exercise: Establishing Your Daily Mindfulness Practice

This exercise will guide you through the process of setting up and committing to a daily mindfulness practice, using the tips and strategies covered in the chapter.

Begin by setting your intention. Take a few moments to reflect on why you want to establish a daily mindfulness practice. What benefits do you hope to gain? What qualities or skills do you want to cultivate? Write down your intention in a journal or notebook.

Next, choose a time and place. Decide on a specific time of day when you'll practice mindfulness meditation. It could be first thing in the morning, during your lunch break, or before bed. Also, choose a quiet, comfortable spot where you can sit uninterrupted for a set period of time.

Remember to start small: Consistency is more important than duration in the beginning. You can always increase your session length over time. Commit to a realistic starting goal, such as meditating for five to ten minutes a day.

Setting reminders is another useful tip that will help you establish a daily practice. Set a recurring alarm or calendar reminder on your phone or computer. You might also leave a sticky note or other visual cue in your meditation spot.

Now, choose your anchor. Decide on a primary focus for your meditation practice, such as your breath, your bodily sensations, or a simple mantra. Having a go-to anchor can help you settle into your practice more quickly and easily.

As you establish your daily practice, remember to practice self-compassion and be kind and patient with yourself. If you miss a day or feel challenged by the practice, simply acknowledge it without judgment and recommit to your intention.

After a week of daily practice, take some time to reflect on your experience. What worked well? What challenges or obstacles did you encounter? What adjustments or tweaks might support your practice going forward? Write down your reflections and insights.

Consider enlisting the support of a friend, family member, or meditation buddy to help keep you accountable and motivated. You could also explore local or online mindfulness communities or resources for guidance and inspiration.

Finally, celebrate your progress. As you continue to show up for your daily practice, take time to acknowledge and recognize your efforts and progress, no matter how small. Remember, every moment of mindfulness is a step on the path of growth and transformation.

Commit to following this exercise for at least one week, and notice how it impacts your relationship to mindfulness practice and your overall well-being. Remember, building a consistent practice is a journey, not a destination, so be patient, persistent, and, above all, kind to yourself along the way.

Chapter 5:

Cultivating Mindfulness in Daily Life

We've learned how to set up a sacred space, find a comfortable posture, and practice some basic techniques like breath awareness, body scans, and mindfulness of thoughts and emotions. We've also explored how to establish a daily practice, including how to gradually increase your session duration, how to overcome challenges, and how to integrate self-guided meditation as your practice deepens. But here's the thing: Mindfulness isn't just something we practice on the cushion. It's a way of being that we can bring into every aspect of our lives, from the mundane to the extraordinary.

In this chapter, we'll explore how to cultivate mindfulness in daily life so that we can live with greater presence, purpose, and joy. We'll look at how to bring mindfulness to everyday activities like eating, walking, and listening, and how to deal with the inevitable distractions and challenges that arise along the way.

Bringing Mindfulness to Everyday Activities

One of the most powerful ways to cultivate mindfulness in daily life is to bring a sense of presence and awareness to the activities we engage in every day. Whether it's eating breakfast, walking to work, or listening to a friend, every moment is an opportunity to practice mindfulness and deepen our connection to the present moment.

Let's start with eating. How often do we sit down to a meal, only to find ourselves scarfing it down while scrolling through our phones or watching TV? When we eat mindlessly like this, we miss out on the rich sensory experience of the food, and we may end up overeating or making poor dietary choices.

Mindful eating, on the other hand, involves bringing our full attention to the experience of eating. We take the time to appreciate the colors, textures, and aromas of the food, and we pay attention to the sensations of hunger and fullness in our bodies. We eat slowly and deliberately, savoring each bite and noticing how the food feels in our mouths and bellies.

To practice mindful eating, try setting aside one meal a day to eat in silence, without any distractions. Put away your phone, turn off the TV, and simply focus on the experience of eating. Notice the colors and textures of the food, the aromas wafting up from your plate, and the flavors exploding on your tongue. Pay attention to the sensations of chewing and swallowing and notice how your body feels as you eat.

Over time, as you practice mindful eating, you may find that you develop a greater appreciation for the food you eat and a deeper sense of connection to your body and its needs. You may also find that you make healthier choices and eat more intuitively, rather than mindlessly overeating or restricting.

Another everyday activity that lends itself well to mindfulness practice is walking. Most of us walk every day, whether it's to get from point A to point B or simply for exercise and fresh air. But how often do we really pay attention to the experience of walking?

Mindful walking involves bringing our full attention to the sensations of our body as we move through space. We notice the feeling of our feet making contact with the ground, the rhythm of our breath, and the movement of our arms and legs. We tune into the sights, sounds, and smells around us, and we allow ourselves to be fully present in the moment.

To practice mindful walking, try taking a short walk each day, even if it's just around the block. As you walk, focus on the sensations of your feet hitting the ground and notice the rhythm of your breath. Pay attention to the sights, sounds, and smells around you and see if you can simply observe them without getting caught up in any stories or judgments.

As you practice mindful walking, you may find that you develop a greater sense of connection to your body and the world around you. You may notice things you've never seen before, like the intricate patterns of leaves on the trees or the way the sunlight dances on the sidewalk. You may also find that walking becomes a form of moving meditation, helping you to feel more grounded, centered, and at peace.

Finally, let's talk about mindful listening. How often do we find ourselves in conversations with others, only to realize that we've been mentally checked out the whole time? When we listen mindlessly like this, we miss out on the opportunity to truly connect with others and understand their perspectives.

Mindful listening, on the other hand, involves bringing our full attention to the person we're communicating with. We put aside our own thoughts and agendas and we simply listen with an open mind and heart. We tune into the tone of their voice, the expressions on their face, and the emotions behind their words.

To practice mindful listening, try setting an intention to be fully present in your conversations with others. Put away your phone, make eye contact, and give the person your undivided attention. Notice any urges to interrupt, give advice, or mentally rehearse your response, and see if you can simply let those urges pass without acting on them.

As you practice mindful listening, you may find that your relationships deepen and become more meaningful. You may develop a greater sense of empathy and understanding for others, and you may find that others feel more heard and valued in your presence.

Dealing With Distractions and Challenges

Of course, cultivating mindfulness in daily life is easier said than done. Our lives are full of distractions and challenges that can pull us out of the present moment and into states of stress, anxiety, or rumination.

But with practice and persistence, we can learn to navigate these challenges with greater ease and grace.

One of the biggest distractions in modern life is technology. Our phones, computers, and televisions are constantly vying for our attention, pulling us away from the present moment and into a world of virtual stimulation. To cultivate mindfulness in the face of technological distractions, try setting aside designated "tech-free" times each day, where you put away your devices and simply focus on the present moment.

You might also try using technology mindfully, by bringing a sense of intention and awareness to your interactions with devices. For example, before checking your email or social media, take a few deep breaths and set an intention to stay present and focused. Notice any urges to get sucked into the virtual world and see if you can simply observe those urges without acting on them.

Another common challenge to mindfulness practice is dealing with difficult emotions like stress, anxiety, or frustration. When we're caught up in these emotions, it can be hard to stay present and focused on the task at hand.

To deal with difficult emotions mindfully, try using the RAIN technique:

- **R**ecognize the emotion that's arising and name it if possible (e.g., "I'm feeling anxious").

- **A**llow the emotion to be there, without trying to push it away or change it.

- **I**nvestigate the emotion with curiosity and openness, noticing how it feels in your body and what thoughts or beliefs may be fueling it.

- **N**urture yourself with compassion and kindness, remembering that difficult emotions are a natural part of the human experience.

By practicing the RAIN technique, you can learn to relate to difficult emotions with greater awareness, acceptance, and self-compassion. You may find that the intensity of the emotion starts to dissipate on its own, allowing you to return to the present moment with greater ease and clarity.

Another challenge to mindfulness practice is dealing with physical discomfort or pain. Whether it's a headache, a sore back, or a chronic illness, physical pain can be a major distraction from the present moment.

To practice mindfulness in the face of physical discomfort, try bringing your attention to the sensations of your body with curiosity and openness. Notice the location, intensity, and quality of the discomfort and see if you can simply observe it without getting caught up in any stories or judgments.

You might also try using your breath as a tool for managing pain. Take slow, deep breaths and imagine the breath moving into and around the area of discomfort. See if you can relax any tension or resistance in your body, and allow the breath to soothe and calm the sensations.

Remember, the goal of mindfulness practice is not to eliminate pain or discomfort altogether, but rather to change your relationship to it. By learning to be present with discomfort with greater awareness and acceptance, you can develop a greater sense of resilience and equanimity in the face of life's challenges.

Cultivating mindfulness in daily life is a lifelong practice, one that requires patience, persistence, and a willingness to show up again and again. It's not about achieving some perfect state of bliss or enlightenment, but rather about learning to be present with whatever arises, moment by moment, with greater awareness and compassion.

By bringing mindfulness to everyday activities like eating, walking, and listening, you can infuse your life with greater presence, purpose, and joy. You can develop a deeper sense of connection to yourself, others, and the world around you and learn to navigate life's challenges with greater ease and grace.

Of course, there will be times when you get caught up in distractions, difficult emotions, or physical discomfort. But with practice and patience, you can learn to meet these challenges with greater mindfulness and self-compassion. You can learn to recognize when you've gotten lost in thought and gently bring yourself back to the present moment.

Exercise: Loving-Kindness Meditation

Loving-kindness meditation, also known as metta meditation, is a powerful practice that helps to cultivate feelings of warmth, care, and goodwill toward ourselves and others. This practice can be particularly helpful when we're feeling stressed, disconnected, or struggling in our relationships.

To begin, find a comfortable seated position, either on a cushion or in a chair. Allow your eyes to close and take a few deep breaths, settling into the present moment.

Bring to mind someone whom you care about deeply, someone who naturally evokes feelings of love and kindness. This could be a close friend, a family member, or even a beloved pet.

Silently recite the following phrases, directing them toward this person: "May you be happy. May you be healthy. May you be safe. May you live with ease."

As you repeat these phrases, allow yourself to really feel the intention behind the words. Imagine the warmth and care emanating from your heart and surrounding this person with love and light.

After a few minutes, shift your attention to yourself. Recite the same phrases, but this time, direct them toward yourself: "May I be happy. May I be healthy. May I be safe. May I live with ease."

Notice any resistance that may arise as you offer these words of kindness to yourself. If you find it difficult, remember that self-compassion is not selfish or indulgent; it's a necessary foundation for extending compassion to others.

Next, bring to mind a neutral person, someone you don't know well but perhaps see in your daily life, such as a cashier at your local grocery store or a neighbor you pass on the street.

Silently recite the phrases of loving-kindness toward this neutral person: "May you be happy. May you be healthy. May you be safe. May you live with ease."

Allow yourself to extend feelings of care and goodwill toward this person, even though you may not know them well.

Finally, bring to mind someone you find difficult or challenging, someone who perhaps evokes feelings of anger, resentment, or hurt.

Silently recite the phrases of loving-kindness toward this difficult person: "May you be happy. May you be healthy. May you be safe. May you live with ease."

Notice any resistance or discomfort that arises as you extend these words of care to this person. Remember that offering loving-kindness does not condone harmful actions or mean that you must have a close relationship with this person. It simply means that you are choosing to let go of ill will and extend a basic level of human care and goodwill to them.

As you finish the practice, take a few deep breaths and notice how you feel. Notice any shifts in your emotional state or your attitude toward yourself and others.

Loving-kindness meditation can be practiced in many different ways: You might choose to focus on one person or group at a time, or extend the phrases of care more broadly to all beings. You can also experiment with different phrases that resonate with you.

The most important thing is to approach the practice with an open heart and a willingness to extend care and compassion to others, even when it feels difficult or uncomfortable. Remember that loving-kindness is not about feeling a certain way, but rather about cultivating an intention of goodwill and care.

As you continue to practice loving-kindness meditation over time, you may start to notice subtle shifts in your relationships and your overall outlook on life. You may find that you're able to extend more patience, understanding, and forgiveness to yourself and others, and that your heart feels more open and connected to the world around you.

Chapter 6:

Deepening Your Practice

You've made it to the juicy part of our mindfulness journey. By now, you've likely established a regular meditation practice and you're starting to see the benefits spill over into your daily life. You're more present, more aware, and more compassionate with yourself and others. But as with any skill, there comes a point where we start to crave more depth, more challenge, and more growth. That's where this chapter comes in.

In the following pages, we'll explore some advanced meditation techniques to take your practice to the next level. We'll delve into the transformative power of loving-kindness and compassion, and we'll talk about how to overcome some of the common pitfalls and plateaus that can arise along the way. So grab your cushion, get comfortable, and let's dive in!

Exploring Advanced Meditation Techniques

As you deepen your mindfulness practice, you may find yourself yearning for new ways to explore the vast landscape of your inner world. While the basic techniques of breath awareness, body scans, and mindfulness of thoughts and emotions are incredibly powerful, there are countless other practices that can help you cultivate greater insight, clarity, and equanimity.

One such practice is called "choiceless awareness." In this technique, rather than focusing on a particular object like your breath or your body, you simply open your awareness to whatever arises in the present moment. You might notice sensations, thoughts, emotions, or sounds, but you don't try to hold onto or push away any particular experience.

Instead, you allow your awareness to rest in a state of open, curious receptivity.

Choiceless awareness can be a powerful way to cultivate a deeper sense of presence and equanimity. By learning to be with whatever arises, without judgment or reactivity, you can start to develop a more spacious and flexible relationship with your inner world. You may start to see that thoughts, emotions, and sensations are simply passing phenomena rather than solid, fixed realities.

To practice choiceless awareness, find a comfortable seated position and allow your eyes to close. Take a few deep breaths, then let your breath settle into its natural rhythm. Notice any sensations in your body, any thoughts or emotions that may be present, and any sounds in the environment around you. Without trying to change or manipulate your experience in any way, simply allow your awareness to rest in the present moment, observing whatever arises with a sense of open, curious receptivity.

If you find your mind getting caught up in a particular thought or feeling, gently redirect your attention back to the totality of your present-moment experience. Remember, the goal is not to achieve some special state or to block out certain experiences, but rather to cultivate a more open and inclusive relationship to whatever is arising in the here and now.

Another advanced technique is called "insight meditation." In this practice, you bring a sense of inquiry and investigation to your present-moment experience. You might ask yourself questions like, "What is the nature of this thought?" or "What is the texture of this emotion in my body?" By bringing a sense of curiosity and openness to your experience, your can start to develop a deeper understanding of the subtle workings of the mind and body.

Insight meditation can be a powerful tool for developing wisdom and self-understanding. By learning to see the impermanent, interconnected, and selfless nature of your experience, you can start to let go of the false sense of separation and solidity that often leads to suffering. You may start to develop a greater sense of freedom, flexibility, and flow in your life.

To practice insight meditation, bring your attention to your breath or another anchor of your choosing. As thoughts, emotions, or sensations arise, turn your attention toward them with a sense of curiosity and investigation. You might silently ask yourself questions like, "What is the nature of this experience?" or "How does this feeling manifest in my body?" Without getting caught up in the content of your experience, see if you can observe it with a sense of open, nonjudgmental awareness.

As you investigate your experience more closely, you may start to notice certain patterns or insights arising. Perhaps you notice how thoughts and emotions are constantly changing and shifting, or how certain experiences trigger habitual patterns of reactivity in the mind and body. By bringing a sense of curiosity and care to these insights, we can start to develop a more wise and compassionate relationship to ourselves and the world around us.

Of course, these are just a few examples of the many advanced meditation techniques out there. Other practices include loving-kindness meditation, compassion meditation, forgiveness meditation, and more. The key is to approach these practices with a sense of openness, curiosity, and willingness to explore. Remember, there's no one "right" way to meditate; the most important thing is to find the practices that resonate with you and support your unique path of growth and awakening.

As you explore these advanced techniques, it's important to remember that they are not a replacement for the foundational practices of mindfulness. Rather, they are a way to deepen and enrich your existing practice, building on the skills and insights you have already cultivated.

It's also important to approach these techniques with a sense of patience and self-compassion. Advanced meditation practices can be challenging, and it's common to encounter frustration, confusion, or doubt along the way. Remember that growth is not always a linear process, and that every moment of practice is an opportunity to learn and evolve.

If you find yourself struggling with a particular technique or experiencing intense emotions or sensations, remember to bring a sense of care and kindness to your experience. It may be helpful to return to a more basic practice, such as breath awareness or body scans, until you feel more grounded and centered.

Ultimately, the goal of advanced meditation techniques is not to achieve some special state or to bypass the challenges of life, but rather to develop a more wise, compassionate, and skillful relationship to ourselves and the world around us. By bringing a sense of curiosity, openness, and care to our practice, we can continue to deepen our understanding and cultivate greater freedom and ease in our lives.

Developing Loving-Kindness and Compassion

One of the most transformative aspects of mindfulness practice is the way in which it can help us cultivate greater loving-kindness and compassion, both for ourselves and for others. When we're caught up in patterns of self-judgment, blame, or resentment, it can be hard to find a sense of peace and connection in our lives. But by intentionally cultivating attitudes of kindness, care, and understanding, we can start to heal these patterns and develop a more loving and inclusive way of being.

One powerful practice for cultivating loving-kindness is called "metta meditation." In this practice, you silently repeat phrases of goodwill and care, first for yourself and then for others. The traditional phrases are:

- "May I be happy."

- "May I be healthy."

- "May I be safe."

- "May I live with ease."

You start by offering these phrases to yourself, really feeling the intention behind the words. Then you extend the phrases outward, to people you love, people you feel neutral toward, and even people you find challenging. You might visualize each person as you offer the phrases or simply hold them in your heart.

Metta meditation can be a powerful way to break down the barriers of separation and judgment that often divide us. By intentionally cultivating attitudes of kindness and care, you start to see the common humanity in all beings. You may find that your heart starts to soften and open, and you develop a greater sense of connection and compassion in your life.

To practice metta meditation, find a comfortable seated position and take a few deep breaths. Bring to mind an image of yourself and silently offer the metta phrases to yourself, really feeling the intention behind the words. You might place a hand on your heart or visualize yourself surrounded by a warm, loving light.

Next, bring to mind someone you love and respect and offer the metta phrases to them. Really feel the warmth and care you have for this person, and imagine them receiving your good wishes. You might visualize them smiling or feeling a sense of peace and happiness.

Then, bring to mind someone you feel neutral toward, such as a neighbor or acquaintance. Offer the metta phrases to this person, recognizing that they, too, want to be happy and free from suffering. See if you can extend a sense of care and goodwill toward them, even if you don't know them well.

Finally, bring to mind someone you find challenging or difficult and offer the metta phrases to them as well. This can be a challenging practice, but see if you can recognize the common humanity you share with this person and extend a sense of care and understanding toward them.

As you practice metta meditation regularly, you may find that your heart starts to open in new and surprising ways. You may find yourself feeling more connected and compassionate toward others, even in challenging situations. And you may start to develop a deeper sense of love and acceptance for yourself, recognizing your own basic goodness and worth.

Another powerful practice for cultivating compassion is called *tonglen*. In this practice, you visualize taking in the suffering of others with each in breath and sending out relief and well-being with each out breath. You might start by connecting with your own suffering and then extend your practice to include the suffering of others.

Tonglen can be a challenging practice, as it asks you to confront the reality of suffering head-on. But by learning to be with suffering in a more open and compassionate way, you can start to develop a greater sense of resilience and empathy. You may find that your heart starts to break open and that you develop a deeper sense of connection and care for all beings.

To practice *tonglen*, find a comfortable seated position and take a few deep breaths. Bring to mind a situation or person that is causing you suffering or distress, and connect with the physical sensations and emotions that arise.

As you breathe in, visualize taking in the suffering and pain of this situation, really feeling it in your body and heart. As you breathe out, visualize sending out relief, ease, and well-being to the person or situation, imagining them being filled with a sense of peace and comfort.

You can then expand your practice to include the suffering of others, visualizing taking in the pain and distress of all beings with each in breath and sending out healing and compassion with each out breath. You might imagine a wide circle of beings around you, all breathing together and sharing in this practice of compassion and care.

As you practice *tonglen* regularly, you may find that your capacity for compassion and empathy starts to expand. You may find yourself feeling more connected to the suffering of others and more motivated to take action to alleviate that suffering in whatever way you can.

Of course, cultivating loving-kindness and compassion is a lifelong practice, one that requires patience, persistence, and a willingness to confront your own patterns of resistance and judgment. But by intentionally bringing these qualities into your life, you can start to create a more loving and inclusive world, one breath at a time.

Overcoming Common Pitfalls and Plateaus

As with any journey of growth and transformation, the path of mindfulness is not always smooth or easy. Along the way, you may encounter various pitfalls and plateaus that can leave you feeling stuck, frustrated, or discouraged. But by learning to recognize and navigate these challenges with wisdom and care, you can continue to deepen your practice and find greater freedom and ease in your life.

One common pitfall is the tendency to get caught up in expectations and ideals. We may have a certain idea of what mindfulness "should" look like, or what kind of experiences we "should" be having in our practice. But the reality is that mindfulness is not about achieving some perfect state of bliss or enlightenment. It's about learning to be with whatever arises, moment by moment, with greater presence and care.

If you find yourself getting caught up in expectations or comparisons, try to bring a sense of curiosity and openness to your experience. Remember that every moment of practice is an opportunity to learn and grow, even (and especially) the challenging ones. Trust that your practice is unfolding in its own unique way, and try to let go of any fixed ideas of what it "should" look like.

One way to work with expectations is to set intentions rather than goals for your practice. Rather than fixating on a particular outcome or achievement, focus on the qualities and attitudes you want to cultivate in your practice, such as presence, curiosity, or compassion. Let go of any attachment to specific results and trust that your practice will unfold in its own natural way.

Another common pitfall is the tendency to get discouraged when we encounter difficult emotions or experiences in our practice. When we start to pay closer attention to our inner world, we may notice painful memories, unresolved traumas, or deep-seated patterns of reactivity that we weren't previously aware of. This can be uncomfortable and even overwhelming at times.

If you find yourself struggling with difficult emotions in your practice, remember to bring a sense of compassion and care to your experience.

Reach out for support if you need it, whether from a teacher, therapist, or trusted friend. Remember that healing is a process, and that it's okay to take things one step at a time.

One helpful approach is to practice "titration" in your meditation practice. This means starting with short periods of practice and gradually building up over time, rather than diving in too deeply too quickly. By working with difficult experiences in small, manageable doses, you can start to build resilience and develop a greater capacity to be with discomfort.

It can also be helpful to balance your meditation practice with other supportive activities, such as physical exercise, time in nature, or creative pursuits. These activities can help regulate the nervous system and provide a sense of grounding and perspective when difficult experiences arise.

Finally, many practitioners experience a sense of plateauing at some point in their journey. We may feel like we're no longer making progress or that our practice has become stale or routine. This is a natural part of the process, and it's important to remember that growth is not always linear or predictable.

If you find yourself in a plateau, try to bring a sense of curiosity and experimentation to your practice. Explore new techniques or approaches, or recommit to the practices that have been most supportive for you in the past. Remember that the goal is not some end point or finish line, but rather a lifelong journey of learning, growth, and discovery.

One way to work with plateaus is to focus on the process rather than the outcome of your practice. Instead of fixating on some future goal or achievement, bring your attention to the present-moment experience of meditation itself. Notice the sensations in your body, the quality of your breath, and the shifting landscape of your thoughts and emotions. By staying curious and engaged with the process of practice, you can find a sense of freshness and aliveness in each moment.

Another helpful approach is to seek out new sources of inspiration and support for your practice. This might mean attending a retreat or workshop, joining a meditation group or community, or working with a teacher or mentor who can offer guidance and encouragement along the way.

Remember, the path of mindfulness is a journey of a lifetime, and there will always be new challenges and opportunities for growth along the way. By approaching these challenges with patience, curiosity, and care, you can continue to deepen your practice and find greater freedom and ease in your life.

The path of mindfulness is a beautiful and transformative journey, one that invites you to show up more fully for your life and for the world around you. As you deepen your practice, you may encounter new challenges and opportunities, but you can trust that each step is an essential part of the process.

By exploring advanced techniques like choiceless awareness and insight meditation, you can start to cultivate a more spacious and flexible relationship with your inner world. By intentionally developing qualities of loving-kindness and compassion, you can start to heal the patterns of separation and judgment that often divide us. And by learning to navigate the common pitfalls and plateaus that arise along the way, you can continue to find greater freedom, ease, and joy in your life.

Remember, the most important thing is to approach your practice with a sense of curiosity, openness, and care. Trust that your unique path is unfolding in its own perfect way and that each moment of mindfulness is planting a seed of greater wisdom, compassion, and peace in the world.

Exercise: Mindful Walking

Mindful walking is a simple yet powerful practice that allows us to bring mindfulness into our daily lives and reconnect with the present moment. This practice can be done anywhere, whether you're walking in nature, around your neighborhood, or even in your own home.

To begin, find a safe and comfortable place to walk, where you can move freely without distractions. If you're walking outdoors, choose a path that is relatively flat and free of obstacles.

Start by standing still and taking a few deep breaths, grounding yourself in the present moment. Notice the sensations of your feet on the ground, the air on your skin, and any sounds or smells around you.

When you're ready, begin walking at a slow and comfortable pace. As you walk, bring your attention to the sensations of your feet making contact with the ground. Notice the weight shifting from one foot to the other, the texture of the surface beneath your feet, and any other physical sensations that arise.

As you continue walking, expand your awareness to include your whole body. Notice the movement of your legs, the swinging of your arms, and the rhythm of your breath. If your mind starts to wander, gently redirect your attention to the sensations of walking.

You might also bring your attention to your surroundings as you walk. Notice the sights, sounds, and smells around you. See if you can maintain a sense of open, curious awareness without getting caught up in any particular thought or distraction.

If you find yourself rushing or hurrying, see if you can slow down and find a more natural, comfortable pace. Remember, the goal is not to get somewhere, but rather to be fully present in the act of walking itself.

As you walk, you might also experiment with different paces and terrains. Notice how your body feels when you walk quickly versus slowly, or when you walk on grass versus concrete. See if you can maintain a sense of mindful awareness throughout these variations.

When you're ready to end your mindful walking practice, come to a gentle stop and take a few deep breaths. Notice how you feel: Is your mind a bit clearer, your body a bit more relaxed? Take a moment to appreciate the simple act of walking and the opportunity to connect with the present moment.

Mindful walking can be practiced for any length of time, from a few minutes to a longer hike or journey. You might start with just five to ten minutes a day and gradually increase the duration over time.

As you continue to practice mindful walking, you may start to notice subtle changes in your relationship to movement and your environment. You may find that you're able to bring more presence and awareness to other daily activities, such as driving, cooking, or even conversations with others.

Remember, the most important thing is to approach the practice with an attitude of openness, curiosity, and nonjudgment. Trust that each step is an opportunity to reconnect with the present moment and cultivate a deeper sense of embodied awareness and presence.

Chapter 7:

Integrating Mindful Meditation Into Your Routine

By now, you've explored the fundamental techniques of mindfulness, delved into some advanced practices, and cultivated a deeper sense of loving-kindness and compassion. You may even have encountered some challenges and plateaus along the way and learned how to navigate them with patience and wisdom.

But as with any new skill or habit, the real test of mindfulness comes in integrating it into your daily life. It's one thing to meditate for a few minutes each day, but it's quite another to bring that same level of presence and awareness to your work, your relationships, and all the other demands of modern life.

In this chapter, we'll explore some practical strategies for weaving mindfulness into your daily routine so that it becomes not just a practice but a way of being in the world. We'll talk about creating a personalized meditation schedule, incorporating mindfulness into your work and relationships, and maintaining consistency and momentum over the long haul.

But before we dive in, let's take a moment to appreciate just how amazing it is that you've made it this far. Seriously, give yourself a pat on the back, or a high five, or a fist bump (or all three, if you're feeling extra celebratory). You've taken on the challenge of cultivating mindfulness in a world that often seems designed to keep us distracted, stressed, and disconnected from ourselves and each other. And you've stuck with it, even when it felt hard or awkward or like you were doing it "wrong." That's a pretty big deal, and it's worth acknowledging.

So, as we explore the art of integrating mindfulness into your daily life, remember to bring that same spirit of self-compassion and celebration to the process. This isn't about perfection or getting it "right"; it's about showing up for yourself and your life with presence, curiosity, and care. And if you can do that, even just a little bit more each day, then you're already winning at this whole mindfulness thing.

Alright, enough with the pep talk. Let's get into the nitty-gritty of how to make mindfulness a regular part of your life, shall we?

Creating a Personalized Meditation Schedule

One of the keys to integrating mindfulness into your life is to make it a regular, consistent practice. Just like brushing your teeth or getting enough sleep, meditation is a habit that requires some level of structure and discipline to maintain.

But here's the thing: There's no one-size-fits-all approach to meditation. What works for one person may not work for another, and what works for you today may not work for you tomorrow. That's why it's so important to create a personalized meditation schedule that fits your unique needs, preferences, and lifestyle.

To start, consider your daily routine and identify some natural gaps or transitions where you could carve out a few minutes for meditation. This might be first thing in the morning, during your lunch break, or right before bed. Experiment with different times of day and see what feels most doable and sustainable for you.

If you're a morning person, you might find that meditating first thing sets a positive tone for the rest of your day. You can start your morning with a few minutes of mindfulness, before you even get out of bed. Just take a few deep breaths, notice how your body feels, and set an intention for the day ahead. It's like a mini pep talk for your mind, without all the cheesy affirmations.

If you're more of a night owl, you might prefer to meditate in the evening, as a way to wind down from the day and prepare for a restful sleep. You can make it part of your bedtime routine, along with brushing your teeth and putting on your favorite pajamas. Just find a quiet spot, sit comfortably, and focus on your breath for a few minutes. It's like a lullaby for your racing mind, without all the singing (unless you want to, in which case, go for it).

But what if you're more of a midday meditator? No problem! You can still find ways to incorporate mindfulness into your workday, even if you don't have a ton of extra time. One option is to take mindful breaks throughout the day—just a few minutes here and there to step away from your desk, take some deep breaths, and reconnect with your body and mind. It's like a mini vacation for your brain, without the sand and sunburn.

The point is, there's no right or wrong time to meditate. The key is to find a time that works for you and to make it a regular part of your routine. And if you miss a day or two (or ten), don't beat yourself up about it. Just start again the next day, with a sense of self-compassion and humor. Remember, this is a practice, not a performance.

Next, think about the length of your practice. While it's great to aspire to longer sits, it's better to start small and build up over time. Even just a few minutes of mindfulness each day can make a big difference in your overall well-being and clarity of mind. And remember, consistency is key—it's better to meditate for five minutes every day than to sit for an hour once a week.

If you're just starting out, you might want to begin with just a few minutes of practice each day and gradually work your way up to longer sessions. You can use a timer to keep track of your practice or just go by your own internal clock. And if you find yourself getting antsy or impatient, just remember that this is a marathon, not a sprint. You don't have to become the Usain Bolt of meditation overnight.

Once you've identified a time and length for your practice, consider creating a dedicated space for meditation in your home or office. This doesn't have to be a fancy meditation room; it can be as simple as a quiet corner with a comfortable cushion or chair. Having a designated space can help signal to your mind and body that it's time to practice, which can make it easier to transition into a state of mindfulness.

Plus, it's just nice to have a little space that's all your own, where you can go to find some peace and quiet in the midst of your busy life. You can decorate it with things that inspire you or bring you joy—maybe a favorite piece of art, a cozy blanket, or a plant that you can watch grow over time. The point is to create a space that feels inviting and supportive so that you actually want to spend time there.

Finally, think about any tools or supports that might enhance your practice. This might include guided meditations, a meditation app, a timer, or a journal for reflection. Experiment with different resources and see what resonates with you.

There are tons of great meditation apps out there, like Headspace, Calm, and Insight Timer, that can help guide you through your practice and keep you motivated over time. And if you prefer a more low-tech approach, you can always just use a simple timer or even a good old-fashioned watch.

The key is to find the tools and supports that work for you, and to use them in a way that feels helpful and sustainable. And remember, you don't need any fancy gadgets or gizmos to meditate; all you really need is your breath, your body, and your mind.

Remember, the goal is to create not a rigid, inflexible schedule but rather a flexible framework that supports your practice over time. Be willing to adjust and adapt as needed, and don't beat yourself up if you miss a day or two. The most important thing is to keep showing up, with patience and self-compassion.

Incorporating Mindfulness Into Work and Relationships

While a dedicated meditation practice is important, the real magic of mindfulness happens when we start to bring it into our daily interactions and activities. By cultivating a more present, aware, and compassionate way of being, we can transform our relationships, our work, and our overall quality of life.

One key area where mindfulness can make a big difference is in our professional lives. Many of us spend a significant portion of our waking hours at work, and it's easy to get caught up in the stress, pressures, and distractions of the job. But by bringing a more mindful approach to our work, we can increase our focus, creativity, and resilience in the face of challenges.

One simple way to incorporate mindfulness into your workday is to take regular mindfulness breaks. This might mean stepping away from your desk for a few minutes to take some deep breaths, or simply pausing between tasks to check in with your body and mind. By creating these small pockets of presence throughout the day, you can help prevent stress and burnout and bring a greater sense of clarity and purpose to your work.

Plus, let's be real—sometimes work can be a total grind. It's easy to get caught up in the endless cycle of emails, meetings, and deadlines and to forget why you're even doing this whole "job" thing in the first place. But by taking a few mindful moments throughout the day, you can reconnect with your deeper sense of purpose and meaning and remember that your work is just one part of the bigger picture of your life.

Another way to bring mindfulness to work is to practice mindful communication with colleagues and clients. This means listening deeply and with full attention instead of getting distracted by your own thoughts or agendas. It also means speaking with intention and care, choosing your words wisely, and communicating in a way that is clear, honest, and respectful.

This can be especially challenging in the workplace, where there are often competing priorities and personalities at play. But by bringing a more mindful approach to your interactions, you can navigate these challenges with greater skill and grace. You can learn to speak up for yourself and your ideas while also being open to the perspectives and needs of others. You can learn to collaborate and compromise rather than getting caught up in power struggles or ego battles.

Mindfulness can also be a powerful tool for navigating difficult conversations or conflicts at work. By bringing a more present, nonreactive approach to these situations, you can respond with greater skill and equanimity rather than getting caught up in the heat of the moment.

This doesn't mean being a pushover or avoiding conflict altogether. Sometimes, difficult conversations need to happen in order for things to move forward. But by bringing a more mindful approach to these interactions, you can communicate your needs and boundaries clearly and respectfully without getting defensive or aggressive. You can listen deeply to the other person's perspective, even if you don't agree with it. And you can find creative solutions that work for everyone, rather than just trying to "win" the argument.

Beyond the workplace, mindfulness can also transform our personal relationships. Whether it's with a partner, family member, or friend, mindfulness can help us show up more fully and authentically in our interactions with others.

One way to cultivate mindfulness in relationships is to practice deep listening. This means giving your full attention to the person you're talking to, without getting distracted by your phone, your thoughts, or your own desire to speak. It means listening not just to the words being spoken but also to the underlying emotions and needs being expressed.

This can be harder than it sounds, especially in our fast-paced, hyper-connected world. It's easy to get caught up in your own thoughts and agendas and to miss what's really being said. But by practicing deep listening, you can create a sense of connection and understanding that goes beyond the surface level. You can show the other person that they matter to you and that you're truly interested in what they have to say.

Mindfulness can also help us communicate more effectively in relationships. By taking a pause before speaking, we can choose our words more carefully and express ourselves with greater clarity and kindness. We can also learn to speak from a place of vulnerability and authenticity rather than hiding behind masks or defenses.

This doesn't mean oversharing or blurting out every thought and feeling that crosses your mind. But it does mean being honest and transparent about what's really going on for you, even when it's uncomfortable or scary. It means letting go of the need to be "perfect" or "right" and instead showing up as your true, imperfect self.

Finally, mindfulness can help us navigate the inevitable challenges and conflicts that arise in relationships. By bringing a more present, compassionate approach to these difficult moments, we can respond with greater wisdom and care instead of reacting out of fear or defensiveness.

This might mean taking a deep breath and counting to ten before responding to a hurtful comment or accusation. It might mean acknowledging your own role in the conflict and taking responsibility for your actions and words. It might mean seeking to understand the other person's perspective, even if you don't agree with it.

Ultimately, mindfulness in relationships is about creating a sense of connection and understanding that goes beyond the surface level. It's about showing up fully and authentically and creating a space where both people can be seen, heard, and valued for who they truly are.

Maintaining Consistency and Momentum

Integrating mindfulness into your life is not a one-time event but an ongoing journey of practice and discovery. Like any new habit or skill, maintaining it over time requires consistency and commitment.

One of the biggest challenges in sustaining a mindfulness practice is dealing with the inevitable ups and downs of motivation and discipline. There will be days when you feel inspired and energized to practice, and other days when you feel resistant or apathetic. This is completely normal and part of the process of establishing any new habit.

To help maintain consistency in your practice, it can be helpful to set realistic goals and intentions. Rather than aiming for some unrealistic ideal of perfect mindfulness, focus on the small, achievable steps you can take each day to support your practice. Celebrate your successes along the way, and be gentle with yourself when you stumble or fall short.

Another key to maintaining momentum is to find ways to stay inspired and engaged with your practice. This might mean attending a meditation retreat or workshop, joining a local mindfulness group or community, or simply reading books or listening to podcasts about mindfulness and personal growth.

It can also be helpful to enlist the support of others in your mindfulness journey. This might mean practicing with a partner or friend, working with a teacher or mentor, or simply sharing your experiences and insights with loved ones. By building a sense of connection and accountability around your practice, you can stay motivated and committed over the long haul.

Plus, let's be real: Sometimes, practicing mindfulness can feel a little lonely or isolating, especially if you're doing it on your own. It can be easy to get discouraged or to feel like you're the only one struggling with this whole "being present" thing. But by connecting with others who are on a similar path, you can find a sense of community and support that can make all the difference.

Finally, remember that mindfulness is not about achieving some end point or goal, but about cultivating a new way of being in each moment. There will be times when your practice feels deep and transformative and other times when it feels shallow or rote. Trust that each moment of practice is planting a seed, and that with patience and persistence, those seeds will bear fruit in ways you can't even imagine.

So keep showing up, dear reader. Keep bringing your full presence and care to each moment, each interaction, each breath. And trust that, little by little, you are cultivating a more mindful, compassionate, and awakened way of being in the world.

And if all else fails, just remember—even the Dalai Lama has bad days. Even the most enlightened among us still struggle with distraction, resistance, and all the other challenges of being human. The point is not to be perfect, but to keep showing up with curiosity, humor, and an open heart.

Integrating mindfulness into your daily routine is a lifelong journey of practice, patience, and discovery. By creating a personalized meditation schedule, bringing mindfulness to your work and relationships, and maintaining consistency and momentum over time, you can weave this transformative practice into the fabric of your life.

Along the way, there will be challenges and setbacks, moments of inspiration and insight, and everything in between. Remember to approach it all with a spirit of curiosity, openness, and self-compassion. Trust that your practice is unfolding in its own perfect way and that each moment of presence is a gift.

As you continue on this path, you may start to notice subtle shifts in the way you relate to yourself, others, and the world around you. You may find that you're more resilient in the face of stress and challenges, more attuned to the needs and feelings of others, and more deeply connected to the beauty and mystery of life itself.

These changes may not happen overnight, but with practice and patience, they will come. And as they do, you may start to discover a deeper sense of peace, purpose, and joy in your life—not as some distant goal to be achieved, but as the very grounding of your being, available in each moment.

And if all else fails, just remember: Mindfulness is not about being perfect, but about being present. It's not about achieving some lofty state of enlightenment, but about showing up for the messy, beautiful, heartbreaking, and hilarious journey of being human.

Exercise: Mindful Movement

Mindful movement practices, such as yoga, tai chi, or qigong, offer a powerful way to cultivate mind–body awareness, release tension and stress, and promote overall well-being. These practices combine gentle physical movements with mindful attention to the breath and the sensations in the body.

To begin, choose a mindful movement practice that resonates with you. This might be a gentle yoga flow, a tai chi sequence, or a qigong routine. If you're new to these practices, you might start with a beginner-friendly class or video to learn the basic movements and principles.

Find a quiet, comfortable space where you can move freely without distractions. Wear comfortable clothing that allows for ease of movement.

Begin by standing still and taking a few deep breaths, grounding yourself in the present moment. Notice the sensations of your feet on the ground, the air on your skin, and any sounds or smells around you.

As you begin to move, bring your full attention to the physical sensations in your body. Notice the stretching and contracting of your muscles, the movement of your joints, and the flow of your breath. If your mind starts to wander, gently redirect your attention back to the sensations of movement.

Move slowly and mindfully, allowing each movement to flow naturally from one to the next. If you encounter any areas of tension or tightness, see if you can breathe into those areas and invite a sense of ease and release.

As you continue to move, notice any thoughts or emotions that arise. See if you can observe them with a sense of curiosity and nonjudgment, without getting caught up in their content. Remember, the goal is not to clear your mind or achieve a particular state, but rather to be fully present with your experience as it unfolds.

If you find yourself striving or pushing too hard, see if you can let go of any sense of effort or force. Allow your movements to be guided by a sense of ease, grace, and flow.

As you near the end of your practice, take a few moments to be still and notice how you feel. Notice any changes in your physical sensations, your emotional state, or your overall sense of well-being.

Mindful movement practices can be done for any length of time, from a few minutes to a longer session. You might start with just 10–15 minutes a day and gradually increase the duration over time.

As you continue to practice mindful movement, you may start to notice subtle changes in your relationship to your body and your mind. You may find that you're able to release tension and stress more easily, both on and off the mat. You may also find that you're able to bring more presence, awareness, and compassion to other areas of your life.

Mindful movement practices offer a rich opportunity to cultivate a deeper sense of embodied presence and well-being. They invite you to reconnect with the wisdom of your body and to find a sense of ease, flow, and joy in the midst of the challenges and complexities of life.

Remember, the most important thing is to approach these practices with a sense of curiosity, openness, and self-compassion. Trust that each movement, each breath, is an opportunity to deepen your awareness and nourish your whole being—mind, body, and spirit.

Chapter 8:

Nurturing Your Mind, Body, and Spirit

We've covered a lot of ground in our exploration of mindfulness meditation. We've learned how to sit still and breathe, how to scan our bodies and observe our thoughts, and how to cultivate loving-kindness and compassion for ourselves and others. We've even talked about how to integrate these practices into our daily lives so that mindfulness becomes not just something we do but a way of being in the world.

But here's the thing: Mindfulness isn't just about what happens on the cushion. It's about how we show up for all the different aspects of our lives—our physical health, our emotional well-being, our relationships, and our connection to the world around us.

In this chapter, we're going to explore some of the ways in which mindfulness can help us nurture our mind, body, and spirit outside of formal meditation practice. We'll talk about mindful eating and nutrition, movement and exercise as meditation, and connecting with nature and community. Because let's face it, we're not just brains on a stick. We're whole, complex, multidimensional beings, and we need to take care of all the different parts of ourselves if we want to live with greater ease, joy, and purpose.

So, grab a snack (a mindful one, of course), put on your favorite pair of stretchy pants, and let's dive in!

Mindful Eating and Nutrition

Let's start with one of the most basic and essential aspects of self-care: eating. We all do it, multiple times a day, but how often do we really pay attention to what we're putting into our bodies and how it makes us feel?

Too often, we eat on autopilot, scarfing down whatever's convenient without really tasting or savoring it. We eat while scrolling through our phones, watching TV, or rushing from one thing to the next. And then we wonder why we feel sluggish, bloated, or unsatisfied.

But what if we approached eating with the same level of mindfulness and care that we bring to our meditation practice? What if we took the time to really be present with our food, to appreciate its colors, textures, and flavors, and to listen to our body's signals of hunger and fullness?

This is where mindful eating comes in. Mindful eating is all about bringing our full attention and awareness to the experience of eating, without judgment or distraction. It's about tuning into our senses, our bodily sensations, and our emotional responses to food, and using that information to make choices that nourish us on every level.

So, what does mindful eating look like in practice? Here are a few tips to get you started:

1. Take a moment to pause and breathe before you start eating. Notice any sensations of hunger or cravings in your body and any thoughts or emotions that may be driving your desire to eat.

2. Choose foods that are both satisfying and nourishing. Focus on whole, unprocessed foods that are rich in nutrients and flavor rather than processed junk that leaves you feeling depleted and unfulfilled.

3. Engage all your senses as you eat. Notice the colors, textures, and aromas of your food. Take small bites and chew slowly, savoring each mouthful. Pay attention to how the flavors and sensations change as you eat.

4. Check in with your body throughout the meal. Notice when you start to feel satisfied and when you feel full. Honor your body's signals, even if that means leaving some food on your plate.

5. Reflect on how you feel after eating. Notice any changes in your energy levels, your mood, or your physical sensations. Use this information to guide your future food choices.

Mindful eating isn't about following a strict set of rules or depriving yourself of the foods you love. It's about developing a more conscious, compassionate relationship with food and your body. It's about nourishing yourself on every level: physically, emotionally, and spiritually.

And the benefits of mindful eating are pretty amazing. Studies have shown that people who practice mindful eating tend to have healthier body weights, better digestion, and more positive attitudes toward food and their bodies. They also report higher levels of satisfaction and enjoyment from eating, as well as lower levels of stress and emotional eating (Nelson, 2017).

But mindful eating isn't just about the individual benefits. It's also about the larger impact our food choices have on the world around us. When we eat mindfully, we're more likely to choose foods that are sustainably and ethically produced, that support local farmers and communities, and that minimize harm to animals and the environment.

So, the next time you sit down to eat, try bringing a little mindfulness to the table. You might be surprised at how much more nourishing and satisfying your meals become—not just for your body, but for your mind and spirit as well.

Movement and Exercise as Meditation

Okay, so we've talked about nourishing our bodies with mindful eating. But what about the other side of the coin: moving our bodies and getting regular exercise?

Now, I know what some of you might be thinking: *Exercise? Ugh. Pass me the remote and a bag of chips.* But hear me out, because when we approach movement and exercise with the same level of mindfulness and intention that we bring to our meditation practice, it can become a powerful tool for nurturing our mind, body, and spirit.

Think about it. When we move our bodies, we're not just burning calories or building muscle. We're also releasing endorphins, reducing stress, and improving our mood and cognitive function. We're connecting with our breath, our sensations, and our inner sense of aliveness. We're challenging ourselves to grow and evolve, both physically and mentally.

In other words, movement and exercise can be a form of meditation—a way of bringing our full presence and awareness to the experience of being in our bodies. And just like with seated meditation, there are many different ways to approach it, depending on your individual needs, preferences, and abilities.

So, what does mindful movement look like in practice? Here are a few ideas to get you started:

- Choose activities that you genuinely enjoy. Whether it's walking, dancing, swimming, or practicing yoga, find ways of moving your body that feel good and bring you a sense of joy and aliveness.

- Set an intention before you start. Take a moment to tune into your body and your breath and set a specific intention for your practice. It might be to cultivate strength, flexibility, or endurance; to release stress or tension; or simply to be present and aware in the moment.

- Focus on your breath and your sensations. As you move, bring your attention to the rhythm of your breath and the sensations in your body. Notice any areas of tension or tightness and any feelings of ease or flow. Use your breath to help you stay present and focused.

- Challenge yourself, but don't overdo it. Mindful movement isn't about pushing yourself to the point of pain or exhaustion. It's about finding a balance between effort and ease and listening to your body's signals of what it needs in each moment.

- Take time to rest and integrate. After your practice, take a few moments to lie down or sit quietly, and notice how your body and mind feel. Observe any shifts in your energy, your mood, or your perspective. Allow yourself to fully absorb and integrate the benefits of your practice.

Mindful movement and exercise can take many different forms, depending on your individual needs and preferences. Some people find that gentle practices like yoga, tai chi, or qigong are the most nourishing and supportive for their bodies and minds. Others prefer more vigorous activities like running, cycling, or weightlifting.

The key is to approach whatever form of movement you choose with a sense of mindfulness, curiosity, and self-compassion. To use it as an opportunity to connect with your body, your breath, and your inner sense of aliveness. To challenge yourself to grow and evolve, both physically and mentally. And to cultivate a deeper sense of presence, resilience, and joy in every moment.

So, if you've been feeling stuck or stagnant in your meditation practice, or if you're looking for new ways to nurture your mind, body, and spirit, consider adding some mindful movement to your routine. You might be surprised at how much more vibrant, energized, and connected you feel, both on and off the cushion.

Connecting With Nature and Community

Alright, my friends. We've explored mindful eating and mindful movement as ways of nurturing our mind, body, and spirit. But there's one more piece of the puzzle that I want to touch on before we wrap up this chapter: the importance of connecting with nature and community.

Now, I know that for some of us (myself included), the idea of "connecting with nature" might conjure up images of hugging trees and singing kumbaya around a campfire. And while there's nothing wrong with a good tree hug or campfire sing-along, that's not exactly what I'm talking about here.

What I'm talking about is the simple but profound act of stepping outside of our own little bubbles and remembering that we're part of something much larger than ourselves; of opening our eyes and our hearts to the beauty, complexity, and interdependence of the natural world around us; and of seeking out opportunities to connect with other human beings in meaningful, authentic, and compassionate ways.

Let's start with nature. There's a growing body of research showing that spending time in nature—whether it's a walk in the park, a hike in the woods, or a swim in the ocean—can have significant benefits for our mental and physical health. It can reduce stress and anxiety, improve mood and cognitive function, and even boost our immune system (Berman et al., 2019).

But beyond the individual health benefits, connecting with nature can also help us cultivate a deeper sense of wonder, awe, and reverence for the world around us. It can remind us of our place in the larger web of life, and of the incredible beauty and resilience of the natural world. It can inspire us to live with greater humility, gratitude, and care for the planet we call home.

So, how can you bring more nature connection into your life? Here are a few ideas:

- Make time for regular nature walks or hikes, even if it's just a short stroll around the block. Notice the sights, sounds, and smells around you and allow yourself to be fully present in the moment.

- Create a nature altar or sacred space in your home, filled with natural objects like stones, shells, or plants. Use it as a place for meditation, reflection, or simply quiet contemplation.

- Get involved in local environmental initiatives, like beach cleanups, tree planting, or community gardening projects. Use it as an opportunity to connect with nature and other like-minded individuals.

- Practice mindful eating by choosing foods that are locally and sustainably grown, and by taking the time to appreciate the natural flavors and textures of each bite.

- Incorporate natural elements into your movement and exercise routine, like practicing yoga outside or going for a swim in a natural body of water.

The key is to approach nature connection with a sense of openness, curiosity, and reverence, allowing yourself to be touched and transformed by the beauty and wisdom of the natural world and using it as an opportunity to cultivate a deeper sense of belonging, purpose, and interconnectedness.

But nature connection isn't just about communing with trees and rocks. It's also about connecting with the human beings around us: our friends, family, neighbors, and community members. Because let's face it, as much as we might like to think of ourselves as independent, self-sufficient individuals, the truth is that we're all deeply interconnected and interdependent.

We need each other—for support, for companionship, for a sense of belonging and purpose. And when we take the time to nurture our relationships and build strong, compassionate communities, we're not just helping others; we're also helping ourselves.

So, how can you bring more community connection into your life? Here are a few ideas:

- Join a local meditation or mindfulness group and use it as an opportunity to connect with others who share your interests and values.

- Volunteer for a cause or organization that you care about and use it as a way to give back to your community and meet new people.

- Host a potluck or community gathering and invite people from different walks of life to come together and share food, stories, and laughter.

- Practice active listening and empathy in your daily interactions and look for opportunities to offer support, encouragement, or a kind word to those around you.

- Seek out diversity in your relationships and communities and use it to learn from and be enriched by different perspectives and experiences.

The key is to approach community connection with a sense of openness, vulnerability, and compassion, to be willing to step outside of your comfort zones and connect with others in authentic, meaningful ways, and to use it as an opportunity to cultivate a deeper sense of belonging, purpose, and interdependence.

Because at the end of the day, mindfulness isn't just about finding inner peace and calm. It's about learning to show up more fully and authentically in all areas of our lives, including our relationships with nature, with each other, and with ourselves.

And when we take the time to nurture these connections, to cultivate a sense of wonder, compassion, and interconnectedness, we're not just improving our own well-being—we're also helping to create a more mindful, compassionate, and sustainable world for all.

We've explored the many ways in which mindfulness can help us nurture our mind, body, and spirit: from the food we eat, to the way we move our bodies, to the connections we cultivate with nature and community. And the beauty of it all is that these practices aren't just about improving our own individual well-being (although that's certainly a big part of it). They're also about learning to show up more fully and authentically in the world and to use our presence and our actions to create positive change and transformation.

Because let's face it, the world can be a pretty crazy, chaotic, and sometimes downright scary place. There's no shortage of things to worry about or feel overwhelmed by, from personal challenges and stressors to larger issues like social injustice, environmental degradation, and political polarization.

But when we cultivate mindfulness in all areas of our lives—when we learn to be present, compassionate, and connected in each moment— we start to tap into a deeper sense of resilience, purpose, and possibility. We start to see that we have the power to choose how we show up in the world and to use our presence and our actions to create the kind of world we want to live in.

So, as you continue on your mindfulness journey, remember to approach it with a sense of curiosity, openness, and self-compassion. Remember that it's not about perfection or achieving some idealized state of being, but rather about showing up fully and authentically in each moment and using that presence to make a positive difference in your own life and in the lives of those around you.

And above all, remember to have fun with it! Mindfulness doesn't have to be all serious and solemn all the time. It can also be playful, creative, and joyful. So, don't be afraid to let your freak flag fly a little and to bring a sense of lightness and humor to your practice.

Because at the end of the day, mindfulness is about learning to embrace the full spectrum of human experience: the joy and the sorrow, the beauty and the pain, the laughter and the tears. It's about learning to be fully alive and awake in each moment, and to use that aliveness to create a more mindful, compassionate, and joyful world for all.

Namaste. Keep shining your light, and never forget how awesome you truly are.

Exercise: Self-Compassion Break

Self-compassion is an essential skill for navigating life's challenges and setbacks with greater resilience and ease. When we're facing difficult emotions, stressful situations, or feelings of inadequacy, self-compassion allows us to turn toward our suffering with kindness, care, and understanding rather than judgment or criticism.

The self-compassion break is a simple yet powerful practice that can be used anytime, anywhere, to bring a sense of comfort, support, and perspective to moments of difficulty.

To begin, take a few deep breaths and bring your attention to the present moment. Notice any physical sensations, thoughts, or emotions that are arising, without trying to change or suppress them.

Now, bring to mind a current situation or challenge that is causing you stress, anxiety, or self-doubt. It might be a difficult conversation, a looming deadline, or a personal struggle that you're facing.

As you hold this situation in your awareness, see if you can acknowledge and validate your own suffering. Silently say to yourself, "This is a moment of suffering. This is hard. This hurts."

Next, remind yourself that suffering is a natural part of the human experience. Silently say to yourself, "Suffering is a part of life. I am not alone in this. Others are struggling too."

Now, place your hand on your heart or another soothing place on your body and offer yourself some words of kindness and compassion. You might say something like, "May I be kind to myself in this moment. May I give myself the compassion I need. May I remember that I am doing the best I can."

Allow yourself to really feel the warmth and comfort of your own touch and your own words of kindness. Take a few deep breaths and let the feelings of care and compassion sink in.

As you finish the practice, take a moment to notice any shifts in your emotional state or perspective. Notice if you feel a bit more grounded, centered, or at ease.

The self-compassion break can be practiced in just a few minutes, anytime you're facing a difficult moment or challenge. You might use it before a stressful meeting, after a difficult conversation, or when you're feeling overwhelmed by self-doubt or self-criticism.

As you continue to practice the self-compassion break over time, you may start to notice subtle changes in your relationship to yourself and your struggles. You may find that you're able to meet difficult moments with greater kindness, patience, and resilience. You may also find that you're able to extend more compassion and understanding to others who are struggling.

Remember, self-compassion is not about avoiding or minimizing your suffering. It's about learning to be with your struggles in a way that is kind, caring, and supportive. It's about recognizing our common humanity and your inherent worthiness, even in the face of life's challenges and imperfections. As you continue on your mindfulness journey, see if you can bring the spirit of self-compassion to all aspects of your practice and your life. Trust that each moment of kindness and care is planting a seed of greater peace, resilience, and well-being, both for yourself and for the world around you.

Chapter 9:

Overcoming Obstacles

We've spent the last eight chapters exploring all the warm and fuzzy aspects of mindfulness meditation: the benefits, the techniques, and the ways it can transform our lives for the better. And don't get me wrong—all of that stuff is great. It's the reason we're here, after all.

But let's be honest: Mindfulness isn't all sunshine and rainbows. It's not some magic pill that will instantly cure all of life's ills and turn us into enlightened beings overnight. Nope, like anything worth pursuing, mindfulness comes with its own set of challenges and obstacles—the kind that can make us want to throw in the towel and go back to our old, unmindful ways.

But fear not, my friends. In this chapter, we're going to tackle some of the biggest obstacles that meditators face head-on. We're going to talk about dealing with resistance and doubt, managing stress and anxiety, and finding the support and accountability we need to stay on track. Because let's face it: If we want to reap the full benefits of mindfulness, we've got to be willing to face the tough stuff too.

Dealing With Resistance and Doubt

First up, let's talk about resistance and doubt—those pesky little voices in our heads that tell us we're not doing it right, that we're not cut out for this whole mindfulness thing, or that we should just give up and go back to scrolling through Instagram.

Sound familiar? Yeah, I thought so. Because here's the thing: Resistance and doubt are totally normal parts of the mindfulness journey. In fact, I'd go so far as to say they're inevitable. After all, we're talking about rewiring our brains and changing deeply ingrained patterns of thought and behavior here. That's not exactly a cakewalk.

But just because resistance and doubt are normal doesn't mean we have to let them run the show. Here are a few strategies for dealing with these common obstacles:

- **Name it to tame it:** When you notice resistance or doubt creeping in, try to identify it for what it is. You might even give it a silly name, like "Doubtful Debbie" or "Resistant Randy." By calling it out and bringing it into the light of awareness, you start to create some space around it—space that allows you to respond rather than react.

- **Get curious:** Instead of trying to push away or ignore your resistance and doubt, try getting curious about them. What do they feel like in your body? What thoughts or beliefs are they pointing to? What might they be trying to teach you? By approaching these obstacles with a spirit of curiosity and openness, you start to shift your relationship to them in a powerful way.

- **Reframe your expectations:** A lot of resistance and doubt stems from unrealistic expectations about what mindfulness "should" look like. We think we should be able to quiet our minds instantly, or that we should feel blissed out and peaceful all the time. But the reality is that mindfulness is messy, imperfect, and often uncomfortable. By reframing our expectations and embracing the full range of our experience, we start to create more space for growth and change.

- **Find your "why":** When resistance and doubt start to feel overwhelming, it can be helpful to reconnect with your deeper motivation for practicing mindfulness. What drew you to this path in the first place? What benefits have you experienced so far? What kind of person do you want to be in the world? By tapping into your deeper "why," you start to build resilience and staying power in the face of obstacles.

Remember, resistance and doubt are not the enemy. They're simply part of the human experience—signposts along the path of growth and transformation. By learning to meet them with curiosity, compassion, and a healthy dose of humor, you will start to develop the inner strength and flexibility you need to navigate life's ups and downs with greater ease and grace.

Managing Stress and Anxiety

Alright, let's move on to another common obstacle that many meditators face—stress and anxiety. Now, I know what you might be thinking: *But wait, isn't mindfulness supposed to help with stress and anxiety? Isn't that kind of the whole point?*

And you're right—mindfulness can be an incredibly powerful tool for managing stress and anxiety. But here's the catch: Sometimes, the very act of trying to be mindful can actually trigger more stress and anxiety. We sit down to meditate, hoping to find some peace and calm, only to be confronted with a tidal wave of racing thoughts, physical tension, and overwhelming emotions.

So, what gives? Well, it turns out that stress and anxiety are actually a natural part of the human experience. They're hardwired into our biology as a way of keeping us safe and alert to potential threats. But in today's fast-paced, always-on world, our stress response can get stuck in overdrive, leaving us feeling chronically anxious, overwhelmed, and on edge.

Mindfulness can help us break this cycle by teaching us to relate to stress and anxiety in a new way. Instead of getting caught up in the content of our anxious thoughts or trying to push away uncomfortable sensations, mindfulness invites us to simply be with our experience as it is, with curiosity and compassion.

Here are a few specific strategies for managing stress and anxiety through mindfulness:

- **Focus on the present moment:** When we're feeling anxious, our minds tend to get caught up in worries about the future or regrets about the past. By bringing our attention back to the present moment—the sensations in our body, the sounds around us, the feeling of our breath—we start to break the cycle of anxious rumination and find a place of greater calm and stability.

- **Practice self-compassion:** Stress and anxiety can be incredibly isolating experiences, leaving us feeling like we're the only ones struggling. But the truth is that everyone experiences stress and anxiety to some degree. By practicing self-compassion—treating ourselves with the same kindness and understanding we would offer a good friend—we start to cultivate a sense of common humanity and resilience in the face of difficulty.

- **Embrace discomfort:** One of the biggest traps of anxiety is the desire to avoid or escape uncomfortable feelings and sensations. But the more we try to push away discomfort, the more power it tends to have over us. By learning to embrace discomfort with mindfulness and curiosity, we start to develop a greater tolerance for the full range of human experience and a deeper sense of inner strength and resilience.

- **Seek professional help:** While mindfulness can be a powerful tool for managing stress and anxiety, it's important to remember that it's not a substitute for professional treatment. If you're struggling with chronic or severe anxiety, it's important to seek the support of a qualified mental health professional who can help you develop a personalized treatment plan.

Remember, mindfulness isn't about eliminating stress and anxiety altogether. It's about learning to relate to these experiences in a new way, with greater awareness, compassion, and resilience. By practicing mindfulness in the face of stress and anxiety, we start to cultivate a deeper sense of inner peace and well-being, even in the midst of life's challenges and uncertainties.

Finding Support and Accountability

Alright, my friends, let's talk about one more common obstacle on the mindfulness path: the need for support and accountability. Because let's face it, as much as we might like to think of ourselves as independent, self-sufficient individuals, the truth is that we all need a little help sometimes.

And when it comes to cultivating a consistent and sustainable mindfulness practice, having the right kind of support and accountability can make all the difference. It can help us stay motivated and on track when we're feeling resistance or doubt, provide a sense of connection and community in the face of isolation and loneliness, and offer guidance and wisdom when we're feeling stuck or confused.

So, what does support and accountability look like in the context of mindfulness? Here are a few ideas:

- **Find a meditation buddy:** One of the simplest and most effective ways to stay accountable to your practice is to find a meditation buddy—someone who shares your interest in mindfulness and is willing to practice with you on a regular basis. You might meet up in person for a weekly sit or connect virtually for a daily practice check-in. Having someone to share the journey with can make all the difference in terms of staying motivated and engaged.

- **Join a mindfulness community:** Another great way to find support and accountability is to join a local or online mindfulness community. This might be a meditation group that meets regularly, a mindfulness-based stress reduction (MBSR) course, or an online forum or social media group dedicated to mindfulness practice. Being part of a community can provide a sense of belonging and connection, as well as access to helpful resources and guidance.

- **Work with a teacher or mentor:** If you're looking for more personalized support and guidance, consider working with a mindfulness teacher or mentor. This might be a one-on-one coaching relationship or a small group program that offers regular check-ins and feedback. A skilled teacher can help you navigate the ups and downs of your practice, offer insights and techniques tailored to your unique needs and goals, and provide a sense of accountability and structure to keep you on track.

- **Create your own accountability system:** Finally, if none of the above options feels quite right for you, consider creating your own accountability system. This might involve setting specific goals and intentions for your practice, tracking your progress in a journal or app, or rewarding yourself for consistent practice with something meaningful and motivating. The key is to find a system that works for you and helps you stay committed to your practice over the long haul.

Remember, cultivating a consistent and sustainable mindfulness practice is a journey, not a destination. There will be ups and downs, challenges and setbacks, moments of inspiration and moments of doubt. But by finding the right kind of support and accountability along the way, you will give yourself the best possible chance of staying the course and reaping the many benefits of this transformative practice.

So, don't be afraid to reach out and ask for help when you need it. Whether it's a meditation buddy, a mindfulness community, a skilled teacher, or your own personalized accountability system, know that you don't have to go it alone. We're all in this together, and by supporting and uplifting each other, we create a ripple effect of mindfulness and compassion that extends far beyond ourselves.

We've explored some of the biggest obstacles that meditators face, from resistance and doubt to stress and anxiety to the need for support and accountability. And we've talked about some practical strategies for navigating these challenges with mindfulness, compassion, and a healthy dose of humor.

No matter how many strategies or techniques we learn, the truth is that obstacles are an inevitable part of the mindfulness journey. They're not something to be avoided or eliminated, but rather something to be embraced as opportunities for growth and transformation. Because when we learn to meet our obstacles with curiosity, openness, and a willingness to learn, we start to develop a whole new relationship to the challenges and uncertainties of life. We start to see that even the toughest experiences can be portals to greater wisdom, resilience, and inner freedom.

So, as you continue on your mindfulness journey, remember to be kind and patient with yourself. Remember that growth is a process, not an event, and that every moment of practice—even the difficult ones—is an opportunity to deepen your understanding and cultivation of this transformative path.

And above all, remember that you're not alone. Whether you're sitting in silent meditation or navigating the ups and downs of daily life, know that you're part of a larger community of mindfulness practitioners all over the world—a community that is here to support you, inspire you, and remind you of your inherent worth and potential.

Exercise: Reflecting on Your Practice

As we've explored throughout this book, mindfulness is not just a one-time experience or a short-term project, but a lifelong journey of growth, discovery, and transformation. By committing to a consistent practice over time, you have the opportunity to cultivate greater presence, compassion, and wisdom in all areas of your life.

One powerful way to support and deepen your mindfulness practice over the long term is through regular reflection and self-inquiry. By taking time to pause and consider your experiences, insights, and challenges, you can gain valuable perspective and clarity and continue to refine and evolve your practice in a way that feels authentic and meaningful to you.

To begin, find a quiet, comfortable place where you can sit and reflect without distractions. You might choose to do this practice at the end of a formal meditation session or as a standalone exercise at another time of day.

Take a few deep breaths and allow your body and mind to settle into the present moment. Bring to mind your mindfulness practice over the past week or month and consider the following questions:

- What have been the most meaningful or impactful moments in my practice recently? What insights, experiences, or realizations have stayed with me?

- What have been the biggest challenges or obstacles in my practice lately? Where have I gotten stuck, frustrated, or discouraged?

- How has my practice been influencing my daily life and relationships? What changes or shifts have I noticed in my thoughts, emotions, or behaviors?

- What do I feel most called to focus on or explore in my practice moving forward? What areas of growth or learning feel most alive and relevant for me right now?

Allow these questions to guide your reflection, without putting pressure on yourself to come up with the "right" answers. Simply notice what arises with a sense of curiosity and openness.

You might choose to journal about your reflections, or simply sit with them in quiet contemplation. You might also choose to share your insights and experiences with a trusted friend, teacher, or community of practitioners.

As you reflect on your practice, remember to approach the process with a sense of kindness, patience, and nonjudgment. Your practice is a living, evolving process, and there is no such thing as a "perfect" meditator or a "finished" journey.

Instead, see if you can approach your reflection with a sense of curiosity, humility, and willingness to learn. Trust that each insight, each challenge, each moment of practice is an opportunity to deepen your understanding and cultivation of mindfulness, both on and off the cushion.

As you continue to reflect on your practice over time, you may start to notice patterns, themes, and areas of growth that emerge. You may find that certain practices or teachings resonate more strongly with you, or that certain obstacles or challenges come up again and again.

By staying committed to regular reflection and self-inquiry, you can continue to refine and evolve your practice in a way that feels authentic, meaningful, and transformative. You can also start to cultivate a deeper sense of self-awareness, self-compassion, and self-trust, which can support you in navigating all aspects of your life with greater clarity, resilience, and ease.

Remember, your mindfulness journey is a unique and personal one, and there is no one "right" way to practice or reflect. Trust your own intuition and inner wisdom and allow your practice to unfold in a way that feels true and nourishing for you.

Chapter 10:

Cultivating a Lifelong Practice

We've reached the final chapter of our mindfulness journey. Can you believe it? It feels like just yesterday we were sitting down to our first meditation, wondering if we were doing it "right" and trying not to get too distracted by that itch on our nose.

But here we are, 10 chapters later, with a whole new set of tools and techniques under our belts. We've learned how to focus on our breath, scan our bodies, and cultivate loving-kindness and compassion. We've explored the benefits of mindful eating, movement, and connection with nature and community. And we've faced some of the biggest obstacles on the path, from resistance and doubt, to stress and anxiety, to the need for support and accountability.

So, what's next? Where do we go from here? How do we take all that we've learned and integrate it into a lifelong practice that continues to nourish and sustain us, even as we navigate the ups and downs of life?

That's what this chapter is all about. We're going to explore what it means to cultivate a mindfulness practice that lasts not just for a few weeks or months, but for a lifetime. We're going to talk about embracing imperfection and growth, celebrating milestones and achievements, and committing to continued learning and evolution. Because let's face it, the journey of mindfulness is never really "done." It's a path that we walk every day, every moment, for the rest of our lives.

Embracing Imperfection and Growth

First things first, let's talk about one of the most important aspects of cultivating a lifelong mindfulness practice: embracing imperfection and growth. No matter how long you've been practicing, no matter how many retreats you've been on or how many books you've read, you're never going to be a "perfect" meditator. And that's okay.

In fact, it's more than okay. It's actually a crucial part of the mindfulness journey. Because when you learn to embrace your imperfections and see them as opportunities for growth and learning, you start to cultivate a whole new relationship to yourself and the world around you.

Think about it this way: Every time you sit down to meditate and your mind starts to wander, every time you catch yourself getting caught up in a swirl of thoughts or emotions, every time you feel like you're "doing it wrong," you're actually being given a precious gift. You're being given the opportunity to practice mindfulness in real time, to bring your awareness back to the present moment, and to cultivate a little more self-compassion and understanding.

And over time, as you continue to practice and embrace these moments of imperfection, something amazing will start to happen. You'll start to see that your "failures" and "mistakes" are actually essential parts of the learning process. You'll start to develop a greater sense of resilience and flexibility in the face of life's challenges. And you'll start to cultivate a deeper sense of self-acceptance and self-love, knowing that you are worthy and valuable, just as you are.

So, as you continue on your mindfulness journey, remember to embrace your imperfections and see them as opportunities for growth. Remember that every moment of practice, no matter how "imperfect," is a chance to deepen your understanding and cultivation of this transformative path.

And when you find yourself getting caught up in self-judgment or comparison, remember this: The goal of mindfulness is not to be "better" than anyone else, or even to be "better" than you were yesterday. The goal is simply to be present, to be aware, and to bring a little more compassion and understanding to each moment of your life.

Celebrating Milestones and Achievements

Let's talk about another important aspect of cultivating a lifelong mindfulness practice: celebrating milestones and achievements. Because let's be real, the mindfulness journey can be a long and winding road, with plenty of ups and downs along the way. And if we're not careful, it's easy to get so caught up in the day-to-day grind of practice that we forget to stop and celebrate how far we've come.

But here's the thing—celebrating our milestones and achievements is not just a nice thing to do. It's actually an essential part of the mindfulness journey. When we take the time to acknowledge and appreciate our growth and progress, we start to cultivate a greater sense of motivation, inspiration, and self-confidence. We start to see that our efforts are paying off and that we really are capable of making meaningful changes in our lives.

So, what does it look like to celebrate milestones and achievements in the context of mindfulness? Here are a few ideas:

- **Keep a mindfulness journal:** One of the simplest and most effective ways to track your progress and celebrate your achievements is to keep a mindfulness journal. This can be as simple as jotting down a few notes after each meditation session, reflecting on what you noticed or learned. Over time, you'll start to see patterns and insights emerging, and you can look back on your journal entries as a way of celebrating how far you've come.

- **Set meaningful goals:** Another way to celebrate your progress is to set meaningful goals for your practice and then take the time to acknowledge and appreciate it when you reach them. This might be something as simple as committing to a daily practice for a certain number of days or setting an intention to bring more mindfulness to a specific area of your life. When you reach your goal, take a moment to celebrate and reflect on what you've learned and how you've grown.

- **Share your journey with others:** Sometimes, the best way to celebrate your mindfulness milestones is to share them with others. This might mean talking to a friend or family member about your practice, joining a mindfulness community or group, or even teaching or sharing mindfulness with others in some way. When we share our journey with others, we not only get to celebrate our own growth and achievements, but we also get to inspire and support others on their own path.

- **Treat yourself:** Finally, don't forget to treat yourself every once in a while! When you reach a big milestone or achievement in your practice, consider rewarding yourself with something meaningful and nourishing. This might be a special treat, a relaxing activity, or even a mindfulness retreat or workshop. The key is to choose something that feels truly celebratory and supports your ongoing growth and well-being.

Remember, celebrating your milestones and achievements is not about ego or self-aggrandizement. It's about taking the time to appreciate and acknowledge the hard work and dedication you've put into your practice and to remind yourself of why you started this journey in the first place.

So, as you continue on your mindfulness path, don't forget to stop and celebrate along the way. Take a moment to appreciate how far you've come and to set your sights on the next milestone or achievement. And above all, remember that every step of the journey—even the challenging ones—is an opportunity to learn, grow, and cultivate a greater sense of presence, compassion, and joy in your life.

Committing to Continued Learning and Evolution

We've reached the final section of this chapter—and, indeed, of this entire book. Can you believe it? It's been quite a journey we've been on together, exploring the ins and outs of mindfulness meditation and how to cultivate a practice that truly nourishes and sustains you.

But as we've discussed throughout this chapter, the journey of mindfulness is never really "done." There's always more to learn, more to explore, more to discover about ourselves and the world around us. And that's why the final piece of the puzzle when it comes to cultivating a lifelong practice is this: committing to continued learning and evolution.

So what does that look like, exactly? Well, it might look different for everyone, depending on their unique interests, needs, and goals. But here are a few ideas to get you started:

- **Keep exploring new techniques and practices:** Just because you've learned the basics of mindfulness meditation doesn't mean there's nothing left to discover. There are countless techniques and practices out there, from loving-kindness and compassion meditations, to mindful movement and breath work, to more esoteric practices like Zen koans and Tibetan dream yoga. Don't be afraid to branch out and try something new—you never know what insights and benefits you might uncover.

- **Seek out teachers and mentors:** One of the best ways to continue learning and evolving in your practice is to seek out the guidance and wisdom of experienced teachers and mentors. This might mean attending a retreat or workshop, working with a one-on-one mindfulness coach, or simply reaching out to a teacher or practitioner you admire and asking for their advice and support. Remember, we all need a little help sometimes, and there's no shame in seeking out the guidance of those who have walked the path before us.

- **Embrace the beginner's mind:** As we gain more experience and knowledge in our practice, it's easy to start feeling like we've "figured it out" or that we know everything there is to know. But the truth is, the moment we think we've arrived at some final destination is the moment we stop growing and learning. That's why it's so important to cultivate what's known as "beginner's mind"—a sense of openness, curiosity, and humility that allows us to approach each moment with fresh eyes and a willingness to learn. So, no matter how long you've been practicing, remember to keep your mind open and your heart curious.

- **Integrate your practice into daily life:** Finally, remember that the ultimate goal of mindfulness is not just to cultivate a formal meditation practice, but to bring the qualities of presence, compassion, and wisdom into every aspect of your life. So, as you continue on your journey, look for ways to integrate your practice into your daily routines and interactions. This might mean bringing more mindfulness to your relationships, your work, your leisure activities, or even the most mundane tasks like brushing your teeth or doing the dishes. The more we can infuse our lives with the spirit of mindfulness, the more we'll start to see the transformative power of this practice in action.

Of course, committing to continued learning and evolution is not always easy. There will be times when you feel stuck, when you encounter obstacles or setbacks, when you wonder if you're really making any progress at all. But that's all part of the journey. And the more you can learn to embrace the ups and downs, the more you'll start to see that every moment—even the challenging ones—is an opportunity for growth and transformation.

So, as you continue on your mindfulness journey, remember to keep your heart open and your mind curious. Remember to seek out the guidance and support of others while also trusting in your own inner wisdom and intuition. Remember to celebrate your milestones and achievements while also embracing the endless opportunities for learning and growth.

And above all, remember that this journey is not about reaching some final destination or achieving some perfect state of being. It's about showing up, again and again, with presence, compassion, and a willingness to learn. It's about cultivating a sense of wonder and awe at the miracle of life and discovering the boundless wisdom and love that lies within each of us.

So, keep practicing. Keep exploring, keep growing, and keep shining your light in the world. And know that, no matter where your journey takes you, you are always exactly where you need to be.

We've reached the end of our mindfulness journey together. We've covered so much ground, from the basics of meditation and mindfulness to the more advanced practices of loving-kindness, self-compassion, and integrating mindfulness into daily life.

We've explored the benefits of mindful eating, movement, and connecting with nature and community. We've faced some of the biggest obstacles on the path, from resistance and doubt to stress and anxiety to the need for support and accountability. And we've talked about what it means to cultivate a lifelong practice, one that continues to nourish and sustain us even as we navigate the ups and downs of life.

It's been quite a ride, hasn't it? The journey of mindfulness is one that lasts a lifetime, and there's always more to explore, more to discover, more to learn about ourselves and the world around us.

So, as you close the pages of this book and step out into the world, I invite you to take a moment to reflect on all that you've learned and experienced. Take a moment to celebrate how far you've come and to set your sights on the next phase of your journey.

Remember, the path of mindfulness is not always easy. There will be challenges and obstacles along the way, moments of doubt and frustration, times when you wonder if you're really making any progress at all. But that's all part of the journey. And the more you can learn to embrace the ups and downs, the more you'll start to see that every moment—even the challenging ones—is an opportunity for growth and transformation.

So keep practicing, my dear ones. Keep showing up for yourself and for others with presence, compassion, and a willingness to learn. Keep exploring new techniques and practices, seeking out the guidance and support of teachers and mentors, and cultivating a sense of beginner's mind and openness to growth.

And above all, remember that you are not alone on this path. You are part of a global community of mindfulness practitioners, all walking this journey together, all working to cultivate a greater sense of peace, joy, and connection in our lives and in the world.

So, thank you for joining me on this journey. Thank you for your openness, your curiosity, your willingness to show up and do the work. And thank you for being a shining light of mindfulness and compassion in the world.

May your practice continue to deepen and evolve, and may you find the strength, wisdom, and love to navigate all of life's ups and downs with grace and resilience. May you always remember the boundless potential that lies within you, and may you never forget the transformative power of this simple, yet profound, practice of mindfulness.

And may you always know, deep in your heart, that you are exactly where you need to be, doing exactly what you need to be doing, in each and every moment.

Exercise: Setting an Intention

As we come to the end of our exploration of mindful meditation, it's important to remember that the journey doesn't end here. In many ways, it's just beginning. The practices, insights, and experiences you've cultivated throughout this book are seeds that will continue to grow and blossom over time as you integrate them into your daily life and ongoing practice.

One powerful way to support this integration and continued growth is by setting a clear and heartfelt intention for your practice moving forward. An intention is different from a goal or a resolution, as it's not about achieving a specific outcome or measuring your progress against external benchmarks. Rather, it's about clarifying the deeper values, qualities, and aspirations that guide and motivate your practice and aligning your actions and choices with those values.

To begin, find a quiet, comfortable place where you can sit and reflect without distractions. Take a few deep breaths and allow your body and mind to settle into the present moment.

Bring to mind your experience with mindfulness meditation so far: the practices you've learned, the insights you've gained, the challenges you've faced. Consider what has been most meaningful and impactful for you and what you feel most called to cultivate and embody moving forward.

Now, take some time to reflect on the following questions:

- What qualities of heart and mind do I most wish to cultivate through my practice? Is it greater presence, compassion, wisdom, or something else?

- How do I want to show up in my life and relationships, both on and off the cushion? What kind of person do I want to be in the world?

- What is the deeper intention behind my practice? Is it to find greater peace and happiness, to be of service to others, to live with more authenticity and purpose?

Allow these questions to guide your reflection, without putting pressure on yourself to come up with the "perfect" answer. Simply notice what arises with a sense of openness and curiosity.

As you reflect, see if you can distill your insights and aspirations into a simple, clear intention that feels authentic and meaningful to you. It might be a short phrase or sentence, such as "May I be present and compassionate in all my interactions" or "May my practice be of benefit to all beings." Or it might be a single word or quality, such as "Peace," "Love," or "Service."

Once you've clarified your intention, take a few moments to sit with it and let it sink in. Notice how it feels in your body and mind. Does it evoke a sense of inspiration, alignment, or purpose?

You might choose to write your intention down and place it somewhere you'll see it regularly, such as on your altar or in your journal. You might also choose to share it with a trusted friend, teacher, or community of practitioners as a way of anchoring your commitment and accountability.

As you continue on your mindfulness journey, see if you can return to your intention often, both in formal practice and in daily life. Use it as a touchstone and a guide, a reminder of what matters most to you and what you're working toward.

Conclusion

We've reached the end of our mindfulness journey together, and what a journey it's been. From the basics of meditation and breath awareness to the more advanced practices of loving-kindness, self-compassion, and integrating mindfulness into daily life, we've covered a lot of ground in these pages.

But as we've discussed throughout this book, the journey of mindfulness is never really over. There's always more to explore, more to discover, more to learn about ourselves and the world around us. And that's the beauty of this practice: It's a lifelong journey of growth, transformation, and awakening.

Reflecting on Your Journey

So, as we close the pages of this book and step out into the world, I invite you to take a moment to reflect on your own mindfulness journey. Think back to where you were when you first picked up this book and all the experiences and insights you've had along the way.

Maybe you started out feeling skeptical or unsure about this whole mindfulness thing, but, over time, you started to notice little changes in your life. Maybe you found yourself feeling a bit more present and aware in your daily interactions, or a bit more compassionate and understanding with yourself and others.

Maybe you had some profound moments of insight or awakening, where you suddenly saw the world in a new light or felt a deep sense of connection and oneness with all beings. Or maybe you had some challenging moments, where you encountered resistance, doubt, or frustration and had to dig deep to find the strength and resilience to keep going.

Whatever your journey has been, take a moment to honor and celebrate it. Recognize all the hard work and dedication you've put into your practice and all the ways in which you've grown and evolved along the way.

And remember, your journey is uniquely yours. There's no right or wrong way to practice mindfulness, and no final destination to reach. The goal is simply to show up, again and again, with presence, curiosity, and an open heart.

Encouragement to Keep Practicing Mindful Meditation

Which brings me to my next point: Don't stop now! The journey of mindfulness may be lifelong, but it's also one that requires ongoing practice and commitment. Just like any skill or habit, mindfulness gets stronger and more ingrained the more you do it.

So, even though you've reached the end of this book, I encourage you to keep practicing mindful meditation in whatever way feels authentic and nourishing to you. Whether it's sitting down for a formal practice each day, taking mindful breaks throughout your workday, or simply bringing more awareness and presence to your daily interactions, find ways to integrate mindfulness into your life on a regular basis.

And remember, there will be ups and downs along the way. There will be days when your practice feels easy and natural and days when it feels like a struggle just to sit still for a few minutes. There will be moments of joy and insight and moments of frustration and doubt.

But through it all, keep coming back to your practice and keep showing up for yourself with compassion and patience. Trust that each moment of awareness and presence is planting a seed, and that with time and nurturing, those seeds will blossom into a greater sense of peace, joy, and connection in your life.

Resources for Further Exploration

Of course, the journey of mindfulness is not one we have to walk alone. There are countless resources out there to support and inspire us along the way, from books and apps to communities and teachers.

So, if you're looking to deepen your practice and continue your exploration of mindfulness, here are a few resources to check out:

Books

- *Wherever You Go, There You Are* by Jon Kabat-Zinn

- *The Power of Now* by Eckhart Tolle

- *Real Happiness: The Power of Meditation* by Sharon Salzberg

- *The Miracle of Mindfulness* by Thich Nhat Hanh

- *10% Happier* by Dan Harris

Apps

- Headspace

- Calm

- Insight Timer

- 10% Happier

- Waking Up with Sam Harris

Communities

- Mindfulness-based stress reduction (MBSR) programs

- Insight Meditation Society

- Spirit Rock Meditation Center

- Shambhala meditation centers

- Zen centers

Remember, these are just a few examples; there are countless other resources out there, and the key is to find the ones that resonate with you and support your unique journey.

And so we come to the end of our time together. It's been an honor and a joy to share this journey with you, and to explore the transformative power of mindfulness meditation together.

As you step out into the world and continue on your own path, remember that you are not alone. You are part of a global community of mindfulness practitioners, all working to cultivate greater peace, compassion, and wisdom in our lives and in the world.

So keep practicing, keep exploring, and keep shining your light. Trust in the journey, and in the boundless potential that lies within you. And know that, no matter where your path takes you, you are always connected to the source of all life, all love, and all wisdom.

References

Berman, M. G., Stier, A. J., & Akcelik, G. N. (2019). Environmental neuroscience. *American Psychologist*, *74*(9), 1039–1052. https://doi.org/10.1037/amp0000583

Cleirigh, D. O., & Greaney, J. (2014). Mindfulness and group performance: An exploratory investigation into the effects of brief mindfulness intervention on group task performance. *Mindfulness*, *6*(3), 601–609. https://doi.org/10.1007/s12671-014-0295-1

Hölzel, B. K., Carmody, J., Vangel, M., Congleton, C., Yerramsetti, S. M., Gard, T., & Lazar, S. W. (2011). Mindfulness practice leads to increases in regional brain gray matter density. *Psychiatry Research: Neuroimaging*, *191*(1), 36–43. https://doi.org/10.1016/j.pscychresns.2010.08.006

Kappen, G., Karremans, J. C., Burk, W. J., & Buyukcan-Tetik, A. (2018). On the association between mindfulness and romantic relationship satisfaction: The role of partner acceptance. *Mindfulness*, *9*(5), 1543–1556. https://doi.org/10.1007/s12671-018-0902-7

Keng, S. L., Smoski, M. J., & Robins, C. J. (2011). Effects of mindfulness on psychological health: A review of empirical studies. *Clinical Psychology Review*, *31*(6), 1041–1056. https://doi.org/10.1016/j.cpr.2011.04.006

Kim, W.-S., Shin, K.-H., & Kim, G.-I. (2014). Differences and similarities in the effects of two meditation methods: Comparing loving-kindness and compassion meditation with mindfulness meditation. *Korean Journal of Health Psychology*, *19*(2), 509–531. https://doi.org/10.17315/kjhp.2014.19.2.004

Manuel, J. A., Somohano, V. C., & Bowen, S. (2016). Mindfulness practice and its relationship to the Five-Facet Mindfulness Questionnaire. *Mindfulness*, *8*(2), 361–367. https://doi.org/10.1007/s12671-016-0605-x

Nelson J. B. (2017). Mindful eating: The art of presence while you eat. *Diabetes Spectrum*, *30*(3), 171–174. https://doi.org/10.2337/ds17-0015

Park, Y., Kim, J.-H., & Kim, M. (2019). The comparison of effects of mindfulness meditation group therapy and mindfulness meditation group therapy added self-compassion meditation for the female patients suffering from chronic musculoskeletal pain. *Stress*, *27*(4), 413–421. https://doi.org/10.17547/kjsr.2019.27.4.412

Phang, C.-K., & Oei, T. P. S. (2012). From mindfulness to meta-mindfulness: Further integration of meta-mindfulness concept and strategies into cognitive-behavioral therapy. *Mindfulness*, *3*(2), 104–116. https://doi.org/10.1007/s12671-011-0084-z

Made in the USA
Middletown, DE
06 October 2024